Microsoft's Hybrid Cloud: Extending the Enterprise Datacenter to Include Windows Azure in the Cloud

Mini-Book Technology Series – Book 2

Authors: Rand Morimoto, Ph.D., MCSE
Chris Amaris, MCITP, CISSP
Guy Yardeni, MCITP, CISSP, MVP

Edited by: Rich Dorfman
Cover Photo by: Noble Henderson

ISBN: 1495942007
ISBN-13: 978-1495942006

DEDICATION

I dedicate this book to my kids Noble, Kelly, Chip,
and Eduardo - Rand Morimoto

I dedicate this book Sophia and our 5 children, Michelle, Megan, Zoe,
Zachary, and Ian. - Chris Amaris

I dedicate this book to Maya Aviv and Zoe Carmel - Guy Yardeni

ACKNOWLEDGMENTS

We would like to thank the following contributors of thoughts, ideas, and examples that resulted in the content throughout this book:

David Kirkman
David Swanson
Manjnath Ajjampur
Subhash Jawahrani
Yoav Land

TABLE OF CONTENTS

INTRODUCTION

For more than two decades, organizations built datacenters and hosted their own servers and systems within their datacenters. The role of the Information Technology (I.T.) department was to keep these systems within their control running in an optimal manner. That included keeping the systems patched and updated, servers and applications backed up, and ensuring all systems were fully operational.

However with the entry of the "cloud", the I.T. departments in organizations are now challenged with a new dimension to I.T. management that includes the management of systems that are not in the four walls of the organization's enterprise datacenter(s). First, it is applications like email, Web conferencing, and file sharing that are being shifted to the cloud. However since full Windows-based guest sessions are now being made available in Infrastructure as a Service (IaaS) hosted environments, organizations have the opportunity to spin up Windows systems in the cloud.

Rather than spinning up Windows-based guest sessions in any cloud environment, Microsoft has made it attractive to spin up Windows-based systems in their Azure in the cloud. The benefits of using Microsoft's Azure cloud services for the virtual machines is the tight integration in what Microsoft has called their CloudOS that matches the operating system on-premise with the operating system in Azure in the cloud.

With the same Windows on-premise and in the cloud, as well as the ability to stretch the enterprise datacenter to include Azure in the cloud, Azure becomes nothing more than an extension to the organization's datacenter. With a stretched network, common hypervisor, and common Windows configuration between the on-premise datacenter and Azure in the cloud, I.T. organizations can truly optimize their ongoing maintenance and support processes with cloud-based resources just like on-premise resources.

This book covers Microsoft's CloudOS strategy and the best practices how organizations are extending their enterprise datacenters to Azure in the cloud, and how organizations can leverage Microsoft's System Center tools for ongoing maintenance, monitoring, management, automation, and support.

1 THE EVOLUTION OF THE TRADITIONAL ENTERPRISE DATACENTER

With the introduction of the personal computer in the early 1980s, organizations started their shift away from the centralized mainframe system with "green screen" terminals to a business environment with individual PC systems. Personal computers gave employees better flexibility and ready access to productivity applications like WordStar, VisiCalc, WordPerfect, and Lotus 1-2-3. However early PCs were all standalone systems that made printer sharing and file sharing a difficult process. It was the rise of Local Area Networks (LANs) that set in motion the traditional enterprise datacenter of today.

Local Area Networks Forming the Basis of Server-based Computing

Early networks in the 1980's from companies like Lantastic and even Microsoft's MSNet started the process of connecting standalone systems together for printer sharing and accessing files stored on each system in peer to peer networking configurations. However it wasn't until 3Com came out with 3+ Share and Novell with their NetWare networking that centralized file sharing started to enter the enterprise environment. Centralized server networking simplified the process where all information was stored in a single location, and thus gave rise to the need for a server closet where these centralized systems were stored.

By the 1990s, more local area network players started to build up market

3

share including IBM with their LanManager based on the IBM OS/2 operating system, Microsoft's version of LanManager based on Microsoft's OS/2, and Banyan Vines.

Mini Computers Along Side LAN-based File Servers

While local area networks focused on file and printer sharing, mini-computers were still the workhorses for business applications like accounting, point of sale, or manufacturing controls. Mini-computers from companies like IBM, DEC, and Sun Microsystems started to replace the use of shared mainframe systems in enterprises. Mini-computers were centralized systems just like the servers in local area networks used for file and printer sharing.

Computer Closets Grow into Datacenters

Organizations that had a single fileserver that was stuffed under a table or in a closet started to realize there was a need for better security, better power protection, and easier backup that could be facilitated by putting all of the servers into a more formal datacenter in their building. The datacenter might not have been a raised floor, temperature controlled room, but at least a room that had more ventilation, battery backup systems, and locked doors or cabinets to provide a bit more security and system protection.

Big Iron Makes Way for Server Racks

For larger enterprises that at one point may have had a mainframe system or a number of mini-computers, the transition to local area network servers mounted in service rack systems transformed the enterprise datacenter from a room with one big system to a room full of server racks. Floor space in datacenters was being repurposed with racks and shelves to accommodate cabling equipment, phone equipment, file servers, and network wiring hubs.

Growth of Application Servers in the Enterprise

By the mid-1990's, a major transition occurred where file servers no longer were used just for storing files, but actual applications were run on the systems. One of the applications that really made a drastic change in the role of the I.T. department and a push toward centralized computing was Microsoft's Exchange email system. Microsoft Exchange was one of the first broadly deployed enterprise focused centralized server applications. Microsoft Exchange was the application that had enterprises shift away from the gold standard of the time, Novell NetWare, to Windows NT, not because Windows NT was particularly better, but it was tied to the Exchange email system.

Other server-based applications also blossomed at the time including Lotus Notes and Oracle's database application server. With the rise of application servers, organizations no longer needed just a centralized file server, but would find itself having multiple file servers, multiple Exchange email servers, and multiple database servers and system that really did start requiring a more formal server rack and centralized datacenter environment.

The Internet Changes Everything

At the same time that application servers were on the rise, the Internet shifted over to being a commercially available connectivity solution for organizations through 56kb and ISDN connections. Once on the Internet, organizations were able to connect their email system to the Internet to send messages between organizations. Additionally, organizations leveraged Internet connections to gain access to content out on the Internet made available through things like Yahoo! search engines from Netscape browsers. Also, with the rise of the Internet, organizations had to make themselves visible on the Internet with a Website presence, so the connection to the Internet provided both an incoming and outgoing connection.

However early Internet connections were expensive, so organizations connected up as many of their server systems and users through single Internet connections, and thus a centralized datacenter model really started to get solidified. Single file servers turned to multiple file servers, multiple application servers, all racked and stacked together and connected out to the Internet.

Viruses, Worms, and Y2K Drive Better Centralized Management

In just a few short years, standalone systems were connected up to networks that were then connected to the World Wide Web with easy access to everything available on the Internet, which also included viruses and worms. The late 1990's welcomed the Melissa worm as well as the changeover into the year 2000.

Enterprises realized they needed to have better centralized management so they could more quickly patch, update, and manage their servers and workstations. Local area network connectivity was no longer just a convenience to gain access to information, but also a way for the I.T department to reach into systems to manage and maintain the systems.

Ongoing viruses like the Blaster Worm and operational changes like the shift in Daylight Savings Time dates in the United States further solidified the need and the standard for centralization, central management, and I.T. operational controls.

Regulatory Compliance Forces Methodical Processes and Enterprise Standards

By the mid-2000's, a whole new set of factors influenced I.T.'s role in centralized management, this time driven by compliance regulations and enterprise standards. Whether it was the Health Insurance Portability and Accountability Act (HIPAA), Sarbanes-Oxley Act, ISO 27001 standards, or the implementation of ITIL standards in an environment, centralized policies, standards, and controls were being implemented in the enterprise.

Systems had to be built, tested, and managed with documented standards, and tighter centralized controls were implemented to ensure system uniformity and compliance. What was simply just connecting systems together to share files and printers a decade earlier had turned into a centrally controlled and tightly managed datacenter environment.

Server Virtualization Opens the Door for Rapid I.T. Expansion

By the late-2000's, server virtualization replaced standalone server systems, so what used to take a day or two to build and configure server hardware and load a single operating system could now be done in a couple hours as a virtual guest session on a host system. Server virtualization led to the ability for an organization to have rapid I.T. expansion of systems, built on the tightly controlled and managed configuration policies and standards derived over the previous several years of standardization.

Managing the Global Enterprise

As we rolled into the 2010's, organizations sought to create global standards, and address global compliance regulations with a well-managed enterprise environment that crossed geographic boundaries around the globe. With over a decade and a half of experience building standard systems, based on specific configurations, to address security and compliance standards, that can be rolled out as virtual guest sessions in an hour or two, the task of I.T. in creating systems was drastically simplified. Focus turned to the management of the system and the automation of processes to assist in the creation, monitoring, management, and support of systems as efficient as possible.

Thoughts and Questions

- Does your organization have documented standards for base configuration of systems in terms of naming standards, standard system setups, and standard configuration settings?
- Does your organization build systems and manage I.T. operations to comply with specific regulatory compliance standards?
- For the most part, are the systems in your enterprise virtualized guest sessions?
- Do you have management tools that provide the organization the ability to monitor and manage systems on a day to day basis?

THE EVOLUTION OF THE TRADITIONAL ENTERPRISE DATACENTER

2 THE ACCEPTANCE OF THE CLOUD IN THE ENTERPRISE

As the datacenter grew out of the closet into a full centrally managed environment influenced by rapid expansion thanks to the Internet and server virtualization, within the first ten years of the 21st Century, the datacenter became the central nervous system of enterprises around the globe. However with the global recession in 2008, the rising costs to maintain, manage, and support the datacenters became a burden on organizations. Chief Information Officers (CIOs) and Chief Financial Officers (CFOs) were looking for a solution to address the year after year growing expenditures of their information systems. It was right at the same time that the "cloud" made its emergence into the marketplace.

The Promises of the Early Enterprise Cloud

As the concept of the enterprise cloud started to catch the media, Chief Information Officers (CIOs) needed to be able to respond that they had a "cloud strategy" being that it seemed like that was key to every (strategic) organization at the time. Products were renamed so that the exact same product a year earlier as an "enterprise business solution" was now rebranded and sold as a "cloud-ready solution". Everything was tagged with the word "cloud" in it.

And with the cloud marketing came the promises: the promise that leveraging a cloud service was cheaper than implementing things in-house. That the cloud was "elastic" meaning that the organization can grow or shrink and only had to buy cloud services for the number of current employees in the organization, no overbuying or under buying hardware devices in-house that were over or under powered. The cloud was to provide organizations "agility" in their growth and expansion as an organization could spin up hundreds of users immediately in the cloud in a business acquisition. The cloud was this amazing thing that did

EVERYTHING!   And of course when CEOs and CFOs heard the advertisements, read very compelling articles in well-respected business and financial journals about how good the cloud was, it was the focus that organizations had to take the cloud seriously.

Early Cloud Adoption Required Patience

But the early cloud was far from actually providing what was promised. Early cloud services were plagued with outages, sometimes lasting an entire business day. The agile pricing sounded great in the marketing materials, but the complexity of calculating data transfer rates, storage rates, computation rates, etc. made the cost hard to calculate and assess the anticipated spend. Most large cloud providers, while having datacenters around the globe, did not provide the ability for organizations to interconnect applications in one datacenter with another datacenter. Each datacenter was isolated in configuration and operations, and thus were independent silos instead of a large broad connected environment. Many cloud providers still have drastic limitations of what they can provide, however those buying cloud services today have more realistic expectations.

Today, you don't get (as many) wild promises as in the past, and buyers are more aware these days, however it took several years before the cloud marketing (and over promises) really settled down. But those that lived through the early days of the cloud were promised more than what they received, and there were some very "exciting" times in those early days.

Shifting to a Services Model in I.T.

As organizations start to "buy" their services from cloud providers, they shift away from a product deployment model to a services consumption model. The organization no longer needs to plan for datacenter space, install server racks, mount server hardware, adjust cooling and electrical systems, buy equipment, burn in hardware, and train administrators on backup and maintenance tasks. As a buyer of services, the requirement is no longer to plan, build, and implement datacenter systems, but rather to purchase the appropriate amount of capacity, and train administrators on the management of cloud-base resources.

There's still a very important requirement to plan, prepare, and train administrators on the consumption of the services, but it's more about remote administration experience focused than the past of building datacenters and systems. The building of the "backend systems" is no longer in the control of the buyer. If a certain level of services are required, then the organization needs to assess the capability of the cloud service provider in meeting those requirements. However in many cases, you get what you get, and you just have to choose to take whatever the service provider provides now and hope the provider will upgrade their services in the future. As cloud providers seek to maintain customers and offer competitive solutions, they are incented to upgrade their service offerings, so the cloud-based solutions are likely to get better over time.

Supply and Demand Become Key

As a consumer of services, the important factor is matching the supply and demand. While some providers charge a flat rate for what most organizations would feel is acceptable service capacity for things like storage, most cloud services are priced on an actual consumption model. Calculations are made to the transaction processes, storage, and transfer of data in and out of the hosted datacenter. If organizations are used to unlimited supply, they may over consume the service in a manner that causes an unnecessary burden of expense. It's similar to a case where if electricity and water were at a flat rate, no one would turn off the lights around the house and everyone would take extra-long showers as there would be no negative consequence for the excessive usage. In these cases, the service would be abused. Some I.T. services, like storage of information, is charged per gigabyte and terabyte, so from a cost perspective it behooves an organization to only store information that is needed, and eliminate content that is not. Or if virtual machines are charged when they are running, but not charged when they are stopped, in test and development environments where dozens of virtual machines are used for testing, the organization needs to turn off systems that aren't in use.

As every economics student learns in school, it is when supply equals demand where cost optimization is achieved. And with lower demand, the consumption is conserved, and costs are driven down further in the organization. As the organization subscribes for services, having methods to optimize the desired capacity for demand will help the organization pay for only the capacity the organization requires.

Buy versus Build

The cloud is not the pinnacle of success for organizations where every workload in the organization needs to be hosted in the cloud, but rather the cloud should be seen as just one additional option the organization can choose to select in their I.T. fulfillment plans. As early adopters to the cloud found, just because cloud services were available early on didn't mean they were reliable enough for the organization, feature rich enough to meet the daily needs of employees, or economical enough to make sense for the organization. With proper strategy planning and a good understanding of the needs of the business, an organization can better determine whether cloud services should be bought on a consumption basis, or whether the organization should build capacity as it has done so for years.

By focusing on what is best to fulfill the needs of the organization, the decision to buy versus build capacity makes more sense. If an organization needs to spin up virtual machines at a rate of dozens or hundreds a day, it may very well be cheaper to build a series of traditional server farms to manage the demand in capacity than to buy services from a cloud provider. However if an organization's development department requires system capacity for sporadic use, and the systems can be shut down when not in use, the organization can leverage the "agility" of the cloud by buying limited services on demand as needed and pay for those services as used.

A new thing organizations also need to add to their thinking about the cloud is whether an all or nothing approach makes sense when making buy versus build decisions. If 80% of the applications in an organization can be moved to a cloud hosted environment, yet for 20% of the applications it makes more sense to use in-house resources, the organization doesn't need to have just a single strategy. Having this flexibility in thinking can allow the organization to best optimize cloud benefits, usually one that includes a hybrid approach that makes the most sense for the organization.

Conversely though, if the organization uses the removal of on premise resources as a deciding factor for cost cutting, yet the organization chooses a "hybrid model" where it remains both on premise and consumes services from the cloud, the organization may find that the decrease in cost it was expecting is not as low as projected, and actually may increase if a hybrid model is chosen. If the organization has to continue to buy and manage servers, licenses, and other resources to retain a "footprint" on premise, the cost associated with the on premise resources plus the monthly cost of the cloud resources might increase the overall cost of I.T. operations.

It's a mathematical calculation that is best done with facts, not with gut feel. Too many I.T. personnel quickly dismiss one model versus another without quantifying what it means to be in one model versus the other for operations. Take email for example, if the organization has 8 email servers today, but chooses to do a split hybrid model where some servers remain on premise and other servers will be migrated to the cloud, while the organization will still have to pay for the cost of on premise resources, if the organization goes from managing and supporting 8 systems across 3 continents for 4000 users to having 3500 users in the cloud and paying monthly for those users, and drop on premise services down to just 1 system in 1 location, there most certainly is a decrease in maintenance and operational cost of on premise services. While it would likely be cheaper to move all servers to the cloud, there is likely still a significant cost savings by moving most systems to the cloud, and hosting just a handful of systems on-premise. Do the math to determine the true cost of build versus buy for the organization in decision making.

Optimizing Supply to Demands

As the organization best understands what it needs for hosted vs in-house systems, the organization can optimize its operational I.T. costs. With some number crunching on various models for build versus buy, the organization can optimize supply to demand. The organization definitely wants to minimize its over purchase of supply if it doesn't use the capacity purchased, and the organization can be more efficient by monitoring and managing user capacity demand and usage, and change practices that can help the organization best optimize costs.

Azure Uptime Compared to Most Enterprises

In looking at uptime of a cloud service like Microsoft's Windows Azure environment, Microsoft guarantees a 99.95% uptime when you deploy two or more role instances in different fault and upgrade domains (http://www.windowsazure.com/en-us/support/legal/sla/). This level of uptime is typically better than what most enterprises can achieve, considering Microsoft has NO regularly scheduled maintenance windows on their environment. You won't get a message from Microsoft that they are doing "maintenance this weekend with a 2-4 hour outage window", that does not happen, so their 99.95% is total uptime including unplanned and planned maintenance and outages.

While it has been a long while since I've heard any of our customers experiencing an outage with Windows Azure services, when Microsoft has service interruption, it might be on a specific series of servers in one of their many datacenters around the world and is limited to a specific group of virtual guest sessions.

Security – Defense in Depth

As for security of Windows Azure, Microsoft has their entire Microsoft Trust Center (http://www.windowsazure.com/en-us/support/trust-center/) where they publish their security standards, and how they address regulatory compliance and privacy protection. Effectively, Microsoft has in place for their Azure services environment a comprehensive Defense in Depth security strategy.

Starting with physical security, Microsoft doesn't provide tours of their datacenters to the public and has very stringent practices leveraging biometric access controls to log everyone who enters and exits their datacenters. Suffice to say, Microsoft's physical security far exceeds the "computer closet" of most small businesses and even the standards for access of most enterprise businesses with the logging, tracking, background checks, and other processes required to be permitted to enter a Microsoft datacenter facility.

Beyond physical security, Microsoft leverages security best practices for connectivity to the Internet that includes no remote access into the host system and networking infrastructure, and has intrusion detection devices implemented.

Flipping around from the datacenter side to the administrator side of Azure, Azure systems are accessed by administrators through SSL-based encrypted sessions. Organizations maintain access credentials to their virtual guest sessions in the cloud, and can enable extensive logging to track access and transactions.

Supporting International Regulatory Compliance

For organizations that have specific regulatory requirements for security that the organization needs to adhere to, Microsoft provides documented statements on their support for things like ISO/IEC 27001:2005, SOC 1 and SOC 2 SSAE 16/ISAE 3402 attestation, PCI Data Security Standards, United Kingdom G-Cloud Impact Level 2 accreditation, HIPAA Business Associate Agreement, Federal Risk and Authorization Management (FedRAMP) authority to operate, and the like. A visit to the Microsoft Trust Center provides an organization updated information supporting Microsoft's compliance around these and other various regulatory compliance standards.

Addressing the Compliance Needs of Enterprises

What I've found over the years is that despite whatever Microsoft publishes as their support for security and compliance standards, the question still comes up, "is my data secure"? And with recent National Security Agency (NSA) leaks about access to information, organizations rightfully have a concern to what level their information is available to others.

For organizations that want to go beyond what is published and committed to by Microsoft for security, there are ways for an organization to own the "keys" for the encrypted content of their organization. For server systems up on Azure, the data on the servers can be encrypted and the organization can own and retain the keys to the encrypted content. A technology that is available within Microsoft's Enterprise Client Access (ECAL) licensing program is Rights Management Services, or RMS. RMS is most commonly used for data leakage protection (DLP) where an organization can have key email messages, files, or other content encrypted to prevent the content from being forwarded to someone else either inside the organization or externally. So even if a server is somehow compromised, the content on the server can only be decrypted by someone with an RMS key who can open the content.

RMS keys are tied to Active Directory user accounts, thus the user (and ultimately the organization) owns the keys to the content that is encrypted with RMS. Even if Microsoft is subpoenaed to release information, the information released will be encrypted blobs of content. A second subpoena would have to be issued to the organization to release the keys to decrypt the content. In this process, the organization will be directly aware that information is being requested to be decrypted, and can seek legal action to prevent the decryption of their content.

Thoughts and Questions

- Does your organization use existing cloud services (like payroll services, Salesforce.com, Office 365, or the like) where cloud services are already accepted within the enterprise?
- Have you done a financial calculation to determine the cost of hosting system services internally (that includes hardware, software licenses, maintenance costs, operational costs, etc.) to determine what a "good price" is for hosted cloud services?
- Do you have regulatory requirements where you'd want to ensure your hosted cloud provider supports specific compliance regulations?
- Would owning and keeping your own keys to data stored at a hosted services provider location give you the comfort level you feel is needed in terms of security and protection?

3 THE EMERGENCE OF THE INFRASTRUCTURE CLOUD

As cloud services have matured and proliferated throughout the industry, the offerings themselves have evolved and expanded. The first examples of cloud services were centered on the "Software as a Service", or SaaS offering. A SaaS application, such as Salesforce.Com, Workday, Yammer or Microsoft's Office 365 is provided to the organization as a complete application with limited control over application configuration and little to no control over the underlying software or infrastructure. Following SaaS, a group of offerings called "Platform as a Service", or PaaS was introduced. PaaS provided the infrastructure and operating system and allowed an organization to deploy its own applications on the provided platform. Web sites, Web services, bulk storage and databases are some examples of application components that can be deployed using a PaaS offering.

The next generation offering provides an organization even more control over the cloud environment while maintaining and improving on the benefits of the cloud platform. Infrastructure as a Service, or IaaS, allows an organization to deploy full infrastructure environments including complete virtual systems, virtual network switches, virtual load balancers and virtual storage. The most advanced offerings, such as Microsoft's Windows Azure environment, offer all three within a single integrated environment. With Windows Azure, SaaS in the form of Office 365, Windows Intune and Windows Azure Active Directory integrates with PaaS in the form of Windows Azure cloud services, Web sites, data services and app services which in turn integrates with IaaS in the form of Windows

Azure virtual machines and network services.

Microsoft's Infrastructure as a Service (IaaS) through Windows Azure

Microsoft Azure launched as a PaaS platform but its current feature set combines IaaS and PaaS features which at times can be confusing as the features are closely integrated within the platform and management consoles. The PaaS features are very powerful and serve specific use cases, such as maintaining development, QA and production environments as part of a development lifecycle management process. However, the full control and flexibility the cloud environment has to offer comes with the IaaS feature set that provides the organization a customized balance between control over deployed resources and their configuration and the simplicity and low cost of maintenance of cloud properties. As use cases demand, the IaaS and PaaS offerings can even be integrated to deliver a cohesive service.

Windows Azure IaaS supports a large variety of existing templates which are pre-configured by the Microsoft Online team. The gallery of templates integrates role specific components with licensing and billing and simplifies rapid deployment of cloud workloads. In addition to the provided templates organizations can deploy custom templates using Microsoft virtual hard disk (VHD) image files, which are typically created using on-premises private cloud environments running Hyper-V. Once virtual machines are deployed in the cloud, whether they originated as a template or as a custom image, they can then be managed using familiar tools and methods. Server configuration, remote access, updating and monitoring can be accomplished using existing and familiar tools. Furthermore, a variety of tools outlined throughout the balance of this book allow for rich integration between the Windows Azure based hosted cloud and the Hyper-V based private cloud in the organization's data center.

Building Virtual Machines in Windows Azure

The process of setting up a new environment in Windows Azure can vary in complexity based on the required configuration but after a short period of familiarity with the tools and options, provisioning can be accomplished rapidly and efficiently. Building virtual machines can be accomplished using the management portal interface, scripted PowerShell commands or the management interfaces provided by System Center.

The creation process using the management portal presents an extensive Windows Azure template library, or Gallery, to quickly deploy systems for a variety of purposes. The gallery templates are created and maintained by the Windows Azure team and includes current Windows server operating systems as well as common application servers such as SQL Server, SharePoint Server, BizTalk and Linux servers running Ubuntu, CentOS or SUSE. A recent gallery upgrade has incorporated templates for Oracle products including Oracle Database, Oracle Linux, WebLogic and Java. Of important note is that gallery templates are license-included which means that the cost for the application license (in the case of SQL, BizTalk and Oracle) is built into the compute cost of the virtual machine and automatically applied to the subscription account while the machine is running.

Regardless of the selected image, the virtual machine's resources are configured based on predetermined system profiles categorized as 'Size'. Sizes available are improved and expanded regularly and currently include 10 types from the 'Extra small' size using a shared core and 768MB of RAM to the 'A9' with 16 cores and 112GB of RAM. Since the costs are based primarily on size, it is important to select the correct size for each VM workload. Given the challenges of a dynamic and evolving workload, the required capacity should be reviewed and adjusted as needed on a regular basis.

The VMs working environment is also configured as part of the creation process identifying the data center region, network environment, availability profile and storage account to host the virtual machine. For virtual machines with large storage or high availability requirements, these settings can have a significant impact and should be carefully planned.

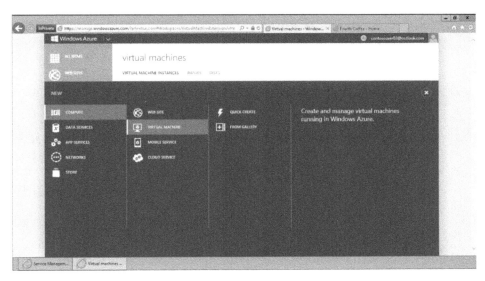

Creating a virtual machine using the Windows Azure Portal

Installing and Running Your Own Applications on Cloud-based VMs

Organizations wishing to have control over the VM templates, adding additional applications or taking advantage or corporate licensing can make use of a provided process to create custom VHD templates on-premises using Hyper-V and then upload those templates for deployment within Windows Azure.

Given the licensing implications of gallery templates and the need for supporting applications not included in the template gallery, most organizations will eventually find themselves on the path to develop, upload and manage images that are customized to the organization. The process to upload a template for use with Windows Azure is not complex and is typically a small leap for organization that already managing a series of private cloud templates, especially when these are Hyper-V/VMM templates.

First, an administrator needs to ensure that the created virtual machine meets the requirements for a Windows Azure virtual machine. Note that these requirements are updated regularly and can currently be found here: http://www.windowsazure.com/en-us/documentation/articles/virtual-machines-create-upload-vhd-windows-server/. Once the requirements are met, the image preparation process will be familiar to anyone who has managed virtual templates or has used the sysprep tool. The prepared image can then be uploaded to a Windows Azure storage account and then imported into the management console as a virtual machine image. Once the image has been published to the Windows Azure virtual machine image repository, it can be used to create a virtual machine like any template in the gallery.

This process can be a very powerful tool for an organization looking to move Microsoft Exchange, Microsoft CRM or other key applications to the cloud. Note that since Windows Azure is an IaaS service, all server management and governance are the responsibility of the organization. Malware protection, backups, security auditing and application high availability are just some examples of critical governance processes that must be addressed for any mission critical service, including those that have been migrated to Windows Azure.

Same Old Application

Often the most time consuming effort in a cloud adoption and migration project is the laborious process of reviewing each candidate application for any architectural or operational modifications that are required to support a cloud deployment. The remediation work can be time consuming and costly, especially for outdated or poorly documented applications. In addition, the resulting solutions are often specific to one cloud provider and can become obsolete as changes to the cloud platform are implemented. This challenging process is commonly a prerequisite before seeing a return on an investment in most PaaS projects and many IaaS projects.

Windows Azure's IaaS platform provides a combination of features that avoids the need for this exercise. The servers provided are not only standard Windows servers running the optimal operating system for the application, they are configured to the same corporate standards as the on-premises servers that host the same workload. With the proper networking and VPN configuration, the same application servers can be relocated between the private and public cloud with minimal application changes and minimal disruption.

The support for applications in their existing code base and with existing configurations facilitates migration projects and provider independence. Organizations can now select to run workloads in private clouds within on-premise's data centers in some instances, while in other cases, the same workload can be deployed to Windows Azure or run in a hybrid mode. Different instances of the same application are commonly deployed this way with development instances running on-premise, test and QA instances in hybrid configurations and production instances on a public cloud where they can easily scale.

Same Old Systems Management

The benefits of running familiar Windows servers in a cloud environment extends to deployment, administration and other IT processes. The existing toolsets and methodologies can be used to deploy, access and manage Windows Azure hosted systems. In many cases, existing processes and procedures can be quickly adapted to support cloud deployments and hybrid deployments using the same toolset and meeting common business goals.

Connected Azure subscriptions can be managed using the provided administration console from any browser-equipped system. For rapid deployment using standards based configuration, PowerShell modules provided for Windows Azure support rapid automated management using existing expertise, current script repositories and PowerShell-based third party tools with minimal modification. Automation platforms such as System Center Orchestrator can also incorporate Windows Azure into existing lifecycle management and governance automation to provide comprehensive governance and management across all systems, hosted or not.

The remote management tool interfaces are automatically configured for new servers in the form of Remote PowerShell and Remote Desktop (RDP) endpoints. The endpoints are provided as entry points for access to each and every virtual machine and deliver seamless remote access for individual system management. Remote Desktop access provides all available server tools that administrators are familiar with including Server Manager and the control panel. These interfaces are all available without any specific network configuration requirements.

With the addition of advanced networking configuration to deploy a site to site VPN between Windows Azure and the on-premises data center, additional configuration options and tools become available. As servers join the same virtual private network as the on-premises data center, they can join the organization's Active Directory. Based on that membership, group policies (GPOs) can be used to manage the servers. As with other servers that are part of the private network, hosted virtual machines can then be managed using management software such as System Center Configuration Manager for software deployment, software updates/patching and other management functions and System Center Operations Manager for alerting and real-time monitoring.

Default management endpoints on a virtual machine

Managing the Operating System and Application Simplifies I.T.'s Experience with the Cloud

The inherent flexibility and integration provided by the SaaS, PaaS and IaaS in Windows Azure provides solutions for most cloud based use cases in most organizations. The implementation approach behind the IaaS offering establishes familiar and easy to use interfaces to existing management and governance systems. This approach reduces the effort involved in all aspects of the system life cycle including deployment, management and administration, migration and support. The Windows Azure solution provides the necessary flexibility across mixed configurations of on-premise, cloud and hybrid based environments. This flexibility reduces the risk and cost of migrating systems to the cloud and supports dynamic hybrid configurations with minimal changes to application code or complex import/export-based deployment processes.

The investment the organization has made in management systems, in employee knowledge and in development of administration processes and procedures is well leveraged in Windows Azure deployments and present a compelling financial argument for many organizations to choose Windows Azure IaaS for their public cloud needs.

Thoughts and Questions

- Do you currently use Remote Desktop Client or Remote PowerShell to access your servers for management and administration?
- Does your organization leverage IT process automation to reduce error, reduce cost and improve service?
- Does your organization have existing management processes and policies that can be modified to incorporate cloud management?
- Does your organization have a business case for partial or full cloud deployment of application environments?

4 MICROSOFT FOLLOWS THROUGH WITH ITS CLOUDOS STRATEGY

When Infrastructure as a Service for Azure Virtual Machine started to take off, Microsoft was on its second or maybe third generation of Windows that was being adapted to the cloud. However, there's a big difference between an operating system being adapted to support the cloud, versus an operating system built specifically for the cloud. Microsoft's CEO at the time, Steve Ballmer, announced Microsoft's Cloud Operating System (CloudOS) strategy in 2008, and Microsoft proceeded to develop its Windows Server operating system to fulfill on this strategy.

The Promise of a Cloud Operating System

As with most tech things in the late 2000's, things were being developed for standalone or on-premise environments and not built to be hosted in a cloud environment. Hosting in a cloud environment requires multi-tenant capabilities where systems can scale to securely support multiple organizations on a single system. When a single tenant solution is put in the cloud, it just doesn't scale to achieve the economies of scale that drives costs down.

Microsoft started its trek to a Cloud-supported operating system with Windows 2008 R2 and then was in full stride with Windows 2012 and Windows 2012 R2. Key features out of these cloud-focused operating systems were the ability to have multiple tenants run applications within the operating system, whether that was in the hypervisor, or Web services, or in its core security model. And, support extended beyond just simple barriers between tenants, but isolation of sessions within the operating system, so that one tenant cannot access files and content, but the actual operating environment that includes memory and core processing isolated between tenants.

Microsoft had a huge benefit over its competitors that were in the hypervisor marketplace because Windows Server was so prevalent in the enterprise business space as an application server environment; plus, Microsoft's Hyper-V virtualization technology integrated into Windows, Microsoft was able to rewrite the operating system to provide functionality from the hypervisor level on up through the operating system and application layers.

Building in System Portability within Windows Server

Another key function built in to the latest version of the Windows Server operating system is the ability to move Windows guest sessions between host servers. In the past, a virtual guest session was tied to a host system, with hooks in the guest sessions for networking, storage, and communications. It wasn't easy to move a guest session from one host server to another and for many virtualization vendors, the connection of the guest session to the host hardware required "clustering" as a method of shifting a system from one host to another. The problem with a clustering model is that it doesn't scale as you can have a 2-way or 4-way or 8-way cluster, but you can't easily have a 100-way, 500-way, or 1,000-way cluster to easily move things around.

Windows Server 2012 broke the barrier between the Windows Server operating system and the underlying Hyper-V hypervisor so that guest sessions can be moved to any other Hyper-V host server through the latest Live Migration functionality in Windows. All processing, memory, networking, and storage functions were isolated within the virtual guest session making it easy to move a guest from system to system. And with pre-staging capabilities of replicating storage content between servers prior to a move, the actual cutover from one host to another is completely seamless to users accessing content on the server. The system can be moved in the middle of the day without dropping connectivity to endpoints.

Selecting to Move a Guest Session from One Host to Another in
Hyper-V

This is the foundation of the latest Windows Server operating system that has provided the backbone for host to host, datacenter to datacenter, datacenter to cloud, and cloud back to datacenter movement of virtual guest sessions.

Maintaining the Basic Platform of Windows Server

While Microsoft built in portability and cloud-focused functionality into the latest releases of the Windows Server operating system, it maintained the basic functionality that organizations have always come to rely on in Windows. There is full support for Windows as a Web server, as a File server, as a domain controller for Active Directory, or as any other Windows-based application server up in the cloud with Windows Azure as has been supported on-premise for years.

The latest Windows Servers can be joined to a domain as well, and applications can be installed, migrated, and configured on the servers. Microsoft made many enhancements to the built-in features in the latest release of Windows Server. Some of the improvements in the latest releases of Windows Server include:

- DirectAccess: Easier configuration and better compatibility support for Microsoft's VPN-less remote connectivity solution.
- File Classification: A built-in function in the file system that can

27

automatically tag and classify files when the content of the file includes confidential information, information that should be tagged as internal only, content that should be tagged as private that might include human resource information, and the like

- Networking Services: Something that is not always top of mind, but are actually valuable improvements are updates in the areas of Windows-based DHCP (for higher availability), DHCP migration tools (that migrate existing DHCP scopes to new servers without interruption of services to services), and better IP management tools.

Utilizing Microsoft Active Directory for User Authentication

For organizations looking to integrate on-premise resources with cloud-based resources, Microsoft's Active Directory remains the authentication mechanism for user access to applications. Through the integration of Active Directory Federation, through the use of a 3rd party single-sign on solution like Ping, Okta, or OneLogin, or by stretching the on-premise network to the cloud, an organization can integrate user authentication from Active Directory.

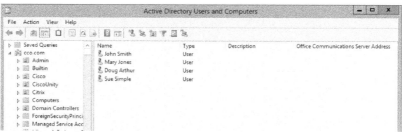

Microsoft Active Directory for User and System Management

For Azure administration, Microsoft still uses a Microsoft LiveID for Azure account and profile information; however within the application on an Azure virtual machine, the system can connect in to Active Directory for user authentication thereafter.

Leveraging Active Directory for Device Authentication and Certificate Management

Active Directory can also be used for device authentication and certification management for servers and systems connected both on-premise and in Azure in the cloud. Systems on-premise and in Azure can be joined to Active Directory with device authentication being managed by

Active Directory. And with Microsoft's Certification Authority (CA), systems that are joined or not joined to Active Directory can have certificates added to the systems for device identification and communications encryption.

Enabling Automated Processes to Equally Provision Systems On-premise and in the Cloud

To create a successful hybrid cloud model, being able to create the exact same guest session in the cloud as has been created on-premise provides the uniformity an organization should expect to maintain enterprise standards for security, compliance, maintenance, and operations. Microsoft provides a number of tools to be able to build standard Windows Server templates that includes something as simple as PowerShell that can be scripted for standard configurations, to System Center where templates can be created and images deployed both on-premise or in the cloud.

Supporting Universal Endpoints – Windows, Macs, Tablets, Mobile Phones

For Hybrid access, Microsoft now provides universal endpoint access for endpoints that include Windows systems, Macs, tablets, and mobile phones. While a server in the cloud may be built on Windows Server, the application running on the server can be configured to support any endpoint.

As an example, an application could be built on the Windows Internet Information Services Web hosting environment that can support HTML, HTML5, Java, .NET, or other Web and application development standards.

And if an application requires the base operating system to be Linux, Microsoft's Hyper-V on-premise as well as Windows Azure in the cloud fully supports running various versions of Linux (SUSE, Ubuntu, CentOS, etc.) as the guest session operating system. Just like running similar Windows templates both on-premise and in Azure in the cloud, Linux templates can be created and deployed on-premise and in Azure for full compatibility in the hybrid configuration model.

Thoughts and Questions

- Does your organization run Windows Server on-premise today?
- If you were to deploy applications in the cloud, would you want to use Windows Server as the base operating system for the applications in the cloud?
- Would having portability of system images and applications between an on-premise datacenter and Azure in the cloud provide better

compatibility and support by having the exact same configurations in the hybrid environment?

- Do you have Microsoft's Active Directory in your environment, and want to tie user and device authentication to Active Directory to consolidate authentication?

5 STRETCHING THE ENTERPRISE DATACENTER TO AZURE IN THE CLOUD

When looking to extend the enterprise datacenter to the cloud, for a fully integrated environment, it's best to have a solid on-premise datacenter infrastructure in place. The more current and solid the on-premise environment is, the better it typically will integrate with the cloud. This is key for an organization in their journey to the cloud.

When the on-premise environment and the cloud environment have different versions of hypervisors, different versions of networking infrastructures, then the connectivity between the on-premise and cloud environment tend to work and operate as independent islands. However when the on-premise and cloud environments are similarly configured, the integration between cloud and on-premise can be more tightly integrated. Obviously the more tightly integrated an environment is, the easier it is to administer and manage, which ultimately drives down the cost of supporting the environment.

Choosing the Hypervisor for the Hybrid Environment

Many enterprises are already using VMware for its hypervisor and the question always comes up whether the organization needs to switch completely to Microsoft's Hyper-V to tightly integrate with Windows Azure in the cloud. The answer is "no" you don't have to completely switch off VMware to Hyper-V; however, if you had Hyper-V, the benefit of similar virtual machine image standards between the on-premise environment and Azure makes the integration of the hybrid cloud model work better with

Hyper-V.

Windows Azure's infrastructure as a service environment is built on Microsoft Hyper-V virtualization. And just as organizations that have both VMware and Hyper-V in their on-premise environments, if you had mixed hypervisors, you know it's not easy to move virtual machines from one hypervisor to the other. Any movement of VMs requires an export and an import, which is very similar to the experience that administrators live through when they are using something like Amazon's cloud for virtual guest sessions. Guest sessions have to be exported and imported across platforms.

So if the organization has Hyper-V on-premise and wants to integrate to Windows Azure in the cloud, the long term integration of the common on-premise and cloud hypervisor would favor the organization having Hyper-V on-premise. That said, if the organization is dead set on keeping VMware on-premise, the organization most certainly can operate with VMware on-premise and integrate with Windows Azure in the cloud.

Leveraging Active Directory for Credential Management

Most organizations use Active Directory on-premise for user and computer authentication, and as such, the organization integrating with Windows Azure in the cloud can continue to use Active Directory on-premise. With Active Directory on-premise, the organization that stretches its on-premise network to Windows Azure can have the Azure-based virtual guest sessions "join" Active Directory across the virtualized network connection. With Windows systems in the cloud joined to Active Directory, just like servers on-premise, the cloud-based servers can be managed, administered, and supported just as if they were on-premise.

Additionally, for applications that'll be installed on Windows Azure virtual machines, the applications can be integrated into the Active Directory for user authentication so that user logons, passwords, group membership, and other AD attributes are tightly integrated.

Benefits of Using Windows Server 2012 R2 Hyper-V as a Base Virtualization Host

As organizations build new virtual machines on-premise, a common question is which version of Hyper-V should be used, whether it makes any difference having an on-premise host server running Windows Server 2008R2, Windows Server 2012, or Windows Server 2012 R2. If you have no particular preference, the recommendation is to build your on-premise guest sessions on top of the latest version of Hyper-V available.

Microsoft has been building in improvements in Hyper-V guest sessions that will provide better performance, better management capabilities, and better high availability and redundancy capabilities with on-premise VMs. One of the capabilities that organizations will benefit from is the ability to replicate virtual guest sessions between on-premise and Windows Azure. Today, Microsoft provides Hyper-V Replica (HVR) between Hyper-V hosts running Hyper-V 2012 R2 guest sessions, and shortly, Microsoft will extend that capability to do HVR between Hyper-V 2012 R2 guest sessions on-premise to Windows Azure (and back).

While Hyper-V Replica to Azure is still forthcoming, other Hyper-V 2012 R2 functionality that is available includes the ability to increase and decrease the amount of memory allocated to a virtual guest sessions, or the ability to expand and shrink a virtual guest session storage on the fly. Also dynamic memory allocation has been part of Hyper-V 2012 that gives an organization flexibility in how much memory is available to guest sessions. While this functionality is a part of the on-premise hypervisor, the benefit of having similar hypervisor on-premise and in Windows Azure is the ability to monitor and manage virtual guest sessions with similar management attributes. As an example, if a virtual guest session on-premise is running out of memory, a management tool like System Center can identify memory usage and a virtual management action can be initiated to increase the memory on the on-premise guest session. And since Windows Azure uses the latest Hyper-V hypervisor, a similar action can be initiated to manage the cloud-based virtual guest session.

Managing Storage On-Premise

When implementing guest sessions on-premise, organizations have the choice of what type of storage system the virtual guests are written to. With the latest Hyper-V 2012 R2 virtual guest sessions, the guests can be written to locally attached disks or to network attached storage, AND the guest session can be booted from either local or network-attached disks. In early releases of Hyper-V, the virtual guest session had to boot to a virtual IDE image on a local disk; however now, a virtual guest session can be a virtual SCSI image that is bootable and can be stored on a network attached disk subsystem. This flexibility provides organizations the ability to store guest sessions either on attached storage or on network storage.

Building a Base Virtual Guest System Session

When building a virtual guest session on Hyper-V 2012 R2, the administrator has the option of creating a Generation 1 or a Generation 2 virtual guest session. Unless there are specific reasons you must use a Generation 1 virtual guest session, it's best to build the guest session as a Generation 2 guest. Generation 2 guests are created as bootable virtual SCSI disks that provide dynamic expansion and shrinking of guest sessions.

It's the latest version of Hyper-V guest standards, so use the latest Generation 2 configuration.

Creating and Using Generation 2 Virtual Machine Types

Also when creating a base virtual guest session, the administrator has the option of creating guest sessions one at a time, or the administrator can create a template that can be reused over and over for future guest sessions. The template configuration is nice in that it simplifies the amount of time it takes for the organization to have a guest session built, especially if a guest session has to be patched or updated with the latest operating system updates. An already patched and updated guest session can be quickly re-replicated with subsequent guest sessions not requiring the update process each and every time.

When working with template guest sessions, the administrator can choose to build the guest session using the Hyper-V console for guest session creation, or use something like System Center Virtual Machine Manager to build the guest sessions. Various options are available that'll be covered later in this book for the automated creation of guest sessions.

Maintaining Status Quo with Existing Applications and Configurations

When creating guest sessions in Windows Azure, the administrators don't need to change their core business applications or treat cloud-based guest sessions drastically differently than on-premise installs of guest sessions. As an example, an IIS Web application that ties to a SQL server backend system typically installs exactly the same on an Azure virtual machine as it does on an on-premise virtual machine. That's one of the big advantages of leveraging Infrastructure as a Service in Windows Azure, the common configuration standards that can be built with on-premise and Azure-based guests.

When installing applications in Windows Azure, a quick validation that the application is supported by the vendor to be installed and placed in the cloud is a prudent step. Some applications, including things like Microsoft Exchange or Microsoft Lync, are not supported right now as Azure virtual guest sessions. Microsoft has their Office 365 offering where Exchange and Lync are offered in the cloud as a SaaS offering, so if an organization is looking for a cloud-based version of those services, Office 365 may be a better alternative.

Microsoft does provide SharePoint as a Windows Azure supported application. Besides SharePoint Online in Office 365, organizations can build SharePoint 2013 and SQL 2012 systems up in Windows Azure as fully supported application systems.

Creating a SQL Server Instance up in Windows Azure

Extending the Enterprise Network to Azure

Once the organization has a solid base infrastructure on-premise and has built appropriate templates and system configurations on-premise, the organization can then extend their on-premise datacenter to Windows

Azure in the cloud. The extension of the on-premise datacenter to Windows Azure in the cloud is the focus of Chapter 6, "Stretching the Enterprise Datacenter to Azure in the Cloud".

Configuring Management Tools to Manage Both On-premise and Cloud Resources

The balance of this book also focuses on the management tools that Microsoft has available to manage guest sessions and applications that are available on-premise as well as in Windows Azure in the cloud. The management tools from Microsoft are part of the System Center family, and has components that help organizations patch, manage, monitor, image, and maintain Microsoft and non-Microsoft based servers, systems, guest sessions, and applications.

Thoughts and Questions

- Are you currently using Hyper-V as your hypervisor, or do you envision any problem shifting to the latest version of Hyper-V as your on-premise host server strategy?
- Do you have Windows server guest sessions and possibly Linux-based guest sessions that you are building on-premise today that you could build up in Windows Azure in the cloud?
- Are you using any version of System Center for administration and management of systems?

6 MANAGING RESOURCES BOTH ONPREMISE AND IN THE CLOUD

As Microsoft developed the Windows Server operating system to be truly portable and universal between on-premise implementations and cloud environments, the next step was to interconnect the traditional on-premise datacenter to Microsoft's Azure in the cloud. This step of "stretching" the on-premise network to the Windows Azure cloud enriches the application, management, and fault tolerance of the enterprise datacenter. Ultimately, it allows organizations to achieve multi-datacenter capabilities without the expense of actually having additional datacenters.

Virtual Machines in Isolated Islands for Operations

As organization begin to move workloads to the cloud, Infrastructure as a Service (IaaS) is an easy point of entry into the cloud service model. Windows Azure provides IaaS capabilities with the Windows Azure Virtual Machines. Organizations can move existing virtual guest sessions or create standalone virtual machines in the Windows Azure public cloud, delivering services such as public facing web servers. The Windows Azure cloud can provide cores, memory, and storage needed for both small and large virtual machines. These isolated workloads typically don't need to communicate with the enterprise network.

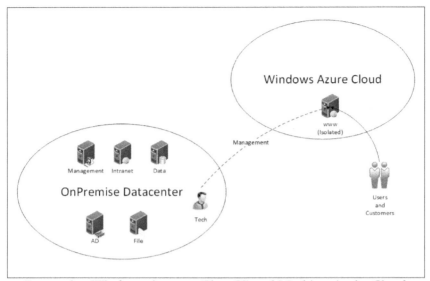

Leveraging Windows Azure to Place Virtual Machines in the Cloud

The isolated workload model typically requires that systems be deployed, configured, secured, patched, maintained, monitored, and backed-up individually and manually. These isolated systems would only provide relatively simple and static services, as they are dependent on local data and can't communicate with back-end databases. However, as the organization gains familiarity with the IaaS cloud services, the workloads become more complex and integration with back-end enterprise data warehouses and enterprise architectures become more likely.

Managing and Supporting Isolated Systems for the Long Run

Managing isolated virtual machines in an IaaS model works in small numbers; but as the organization begins to scale up the number of workloads, the burden of maintaining these workloads scales linearly or even exponentially. This is similar to the early days of standalone PC's, where maintaining the PC's required technicians to walk around to each system to install software or provide maintenance. As the deployment of PC's scaled up, the industry developed and organizations deployed enterprise class management tools to provide deployment management, policy management, security management, and patch management. This required that the PC's be networked to a central location to provide those management services.

Similarly, as organizations deploy more and more isolated virtual machines to the IaaS cloud, the pressure mounts to provide enterprise class management tools. These tools are already deployed in the organization's on-premise datacenter, managing the on-premise workloads. This provides a natural progression for the organization to want to stretch the enterprise datacenter to the Windows Azure IaaS cloud and allow the enterprise management tools to manage the Windows Azure cloud workloads.

A good rule of thumb is if the number of isolated virtual machines in the cloud is more than the digits on one hand, then it's time to consider using enterprise management tools.

Directly Building and Transferring Versus Importing and Exporting Virtual Machines

When organizations first begin using Windows Azure Virtual Machines, it is easy to create the virtual machines using a platform image from the Windows Azure image gallery. There are a number of different generic workload images available. This provides a quick and simple method of creating a generic cloud workload that can then be manually customized as needed.

As an organization begins to scale out the Windows Azure environment, it becomes more important to standardize the isolated virtual machines to reduce variance and ease the administration burden. There is also a natural push to reduce the manual steps needed to customize a given workload, both to reduce the level of effort to deploy and reduce the time-to-market for a given virtual machine. This provides a natural incentive to deploy a customized platform image rather than a generic platform image.

In contrast to other cloud providers, Windows Azure Virtual Machines provide the capability to both build VMs out of a Microsoft supplied template library, or to create your own virtual guest image. Easy to use tools like the CSUpload tool from the Windows Azure Software Development Kit (SDK) allow organizations to easily upload their custom images and then deploy new virtual machines in the Windows Azure IaaS cloud using those custom images, reducing the level of effort needed to deploy the organization-specific workloads and also the time-to-market for those workloads.

Introducing Network Virtualization Between On-premise Datacenters and the Cloud

Scaling up the organizations IaaS cloud footprint brings pressures to provide enterprise level management and enterprise integrations. The relief of these pressures was addressed in network virtualization and stretching the on-premise datacenter into the IaaS cloud. The Windows Azure Virtual Network allows organizations to stretch their datacenters into the Windows

Azure IaaS cloud using Virtual Private Networking (VPN) technologies.

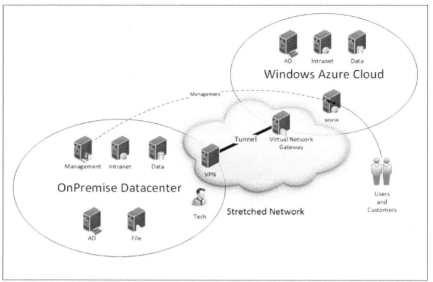

Stretching an Enterprise Datacenter to Include Azure VMs in the Cloud

VPNs allow the extension of the on-premise datacenter to the IaaS cloud using a highly secure tunnel, using advanced authentication and encryption to protect the confidentiality of the connections. The Windows Azure Virtual Network supports a wide variety of devices from major vendors such as Cisco, Juniper, Watchguard, F5, Citrix, and Microsoft, so Windows Azure allows organizations flexibility in establishing the VPN connections.

The network virtualization allows the on-premise enterprise management system such as System Center 2012 R2 to extended its management to Windows Azure Virtual Machines and bring the organization's IaaS under the management umbrella. The allows the formerly isolated IaaS cloud workloads to be managed, monitored, and maintained as first class enterprise citizens, dramatically reducing the level of effort needed to support the cloud systems.

It also allows the Windows Azure Virtual Machines to securely integrate with the on-premise systems to provide real-time access to data and provide higher quality services. This could include accessing data warehouses and enterprise systems for the most current information. This provides the opportunity to deploy richer, more sophisticated, and more dynamic services in the IaaS cloud.

Extending Network Virtualization Across Private and Public Cloud Datacenters

The extension of the datacenter to the Azure cloud using network virtualization can also be extended to 3rd Party Hosted clouds or subsidiary datacenters. This extension of the on-premise private cloud to the Azure cloud, 3rd party clouds, and subsidiary datacenters provides the flexibility to move workloads to wherever it makes the most sense while maintaining full connectivity and functionality.

This allows workloads to be executed where it makes the most sense from a cost and performance perspective. For example, during development, an application workload might be hosted in the Windows Azure cloud to provide rapid provisioning and de-provisioning of lab workloads for testing. During quality assurance, the application workloads might be located in a 3rd party hosted cloud. And finally, during the production deployment the application workloads might be located in both the on-premise datacenter and the Windows Azure cloud.

Workloads can also be seamlessly moved from the on-premise datacenter private cloud to the Windows Azure public cloud; or additional nodes in a system can be created in the Windows Azure public cloud and integrated automatically into on-premise systems. This could be for high availability or for performance, allowing organizations to "burst" to the cloud during periods of peak loads and then draw down the workloads once the peak period has passed.

The network virtualization and the stretching of the datacenter to other clouds provides organizations the flexibility to move virtual machines and applications between the private or public cloud, wherever it makes the most sense for the organization.

Accessing and Managing Virtual Machines on a Stretched Network

Because resources on a stretched network are within the security boundary of the on-premise network, standard methods of access can be used to work with these resources. The virtual machines are accessible via standard TCP/IP networking, allowing them to be accessed in the same fashion as the on-premise datacenter systems. This includes tools such as Ping for testing connectivity, Remote Desktop Connection (RDC) for accessing the console remotely, PowerShell Remote for running scripts, and Server Message Block (SMB) for file transfers.

This allows administrators the ability to manage and maintain the systems across a stretched network without regard to the location of the systems. The location of any given workload is transparent to the management of the workload, much the same way that management of physical and virtual systems is transparent to the administrator. This avoids the need for special techniques, training, or trouble managing machines in the Windows Azure IaaS cloud with a stretched network.

For more details on the tools, see Chapter 7 "Managing Resources Both On-premise and In the Cloud", which covers the tools for managing virtual machines in the public and private cloud.

Supporting Data Replication Between Datacenters

Similar to the tools transparency with a stretched network, data replication is also transparent on a stretched network. Modern networks implement a number of data replication techniques, from Active Directory replication to SQL Always On replication. The stretched network allows for those replication technologies to be extended into the Windows Azure cloud.

Since the stretched network model provides seamless access between resources in the on-premise datacenter and the Windows Azure cloud, the same replication techniques used between the organization's on-premise datacenters can be used to replicate to the Windows Azure IaaS cloud. For example, Active Directory domain controllers can be placed in the Windows Azure cloud with a stretched network and the domain controller will synchronize back and forth. The same is true for SQL Always On replication, which allows SQL databases to be replicated from the on-premise data center to the Windows Azure cloud.

It is important to factor in network performance into the decision to replicate into the Windows Azure cloud. Bandwidth availability, latency of the links, size of the replicated data, and the rate of change of the data will all influence the replication time. For example, a high transaction system will have a high rate of data change, which will in turn generate a larger set of data to be replicated and thus require larger network connections to accommodate the replication.

Managing High Availability and Redundancy Between Datacenters

When the on-premise datacenter is stretched to the Windows Azure IaaS cloud, it opens up new possibilities for organizations to provide high availability and redundancy. The ability to seamlessly replicate data and workloads into the cloud and back on-premise provides options to make application highly available through redundancy. The Windows Azure IaaS cloud can provide geographical fault tolerance with Windows Azure Geo-Replication. The systems and data hosted in the Windows Azure cloud are automatically replicated to a secondary Windows Azure datacenter geographically distant from the primary Windows Azure datacenter. This ensures that even if there is a regional disaster, the Windows Azure workload will continue to provide services.

The high availability of the stretched datacenter can take two different forms, either warm standby or hot active systems in the Windows Azure cloud. With warm standby systems, the data can be passively replicated to the cloud systems. In the event of a disaster in the on-premise datacenter, the Windows Azure warm standby systems can be made active and provide an immediate resumption of services.

With hot active systems, the Windows Azure systems are active and load balanced with the on-premise data center. In the event of a datacenter outage, the Windows Azure systems will seamlessly continue to provide services. This ensures true high availability and zero downtime in the event of an on-premise datacenter disaster.

The stretched on-premise datacenter allows organizations with a single datacenter to achieve the global high availability previously only attainable though the expensive deployment of multiple data centers in different geographic regions without all the headaches, staffing, and maintenance overhead. Windows Azure Virtual Machines and Windows Azure Virtual Network gives organizations an easy path to achieve true high availability for their systems.

Thoughts and Questions

- Which workloads can run as isolated systems? These will be good candidates for early migration to Windows Azure Virtual Machines.

- Will stretching the on-premise datacenter allow for key scenarios such as enterprise level management of cloud systems and rich integration with on-premise systems?

- Which workloads require connections to on-premise databases or systems? These will be better candidates to migrate after stretching the on-premise datacenter to the cloud.

- When will the number of workloads in the Windows Azure IaaS cloud require enterprise management tools?

- Has there been a review of data volume and rates of change of data to make an informed decision what to replicate to Windows Azure?

- What are the mission critical systems in the organization that would benefit from stretched datacenter and geographic high availability?

7 HOLISTICALLY MONITORING THE HYBRID ENTERPRISE

For the past 5-10 years, we've seen a shift from physical servers to virtual guest session systems that has drastically changed the way datacenters facilitate application services. The latest shift has been stretching networks using network virtualization as was covered in Chapter 6. Until Microsoft included network virtualization right within Windows Server 2012 R2, organizations either had to buy hardware appliances to stretch networks to the cloud or in many cases had to manage cloud-based virtual machines as completely isolated systems. However, for organizations that interconnect their on-premise datacenters to Windows Azure, cloud-based virtual machines are now seen as if they are right on the enterprise local network. IT departments know how to manage local systems, and thus network virtualization greatly simplifies the task of managing and supporting virtual machines residing both on-premise and in the cloud.

Utilizing Built-in Windows Management Tools

To manage systems, Microsoft provides a number of tools right within the Windows Server operating system itself. These tools include Server Manager, Windows PowerShell, Performance Monitor (PerfMon), and Remote Desktop Console. The tools have been updated over the past several releases of Windows Server, so if it has been a while since you've used them, you may want to take a look at the latest releases of the tools.

Leveraging Server Manager in Windows Server 2012 R2

Server Manager is the latest console Microsoft released with Windows Server 2012 and has been expanded in Windows Server 2012 R2. Server Manager includes a single view of all of the various Windows Server management consoles including server views into clustering consoles, Remote Desktop Services consoles, Storage Spaces, Performance Monitoring, and the like. Rather than having to launch multiple administration consoles or configure multiple servers individually, Server Manager allows an administrator to connect to multiple host systems, configure all of the systems at the same time, and monitor and manage resources for the server based applications.

Microsoft Server Manager for Centralized System Management

A common example of Server Manager consolidation is if you want to make a handful of systems into Hyper-V host servers. Rather than logging in to each host server and "Add a Role" to each server, Server Manager allows you to select multiple systems and add the Hyper-V Services role to all servers at the same time. Another common use of Server Manager is to create shared stores across multiple systems using Storage Spaces. Rather than going to multiple servers individually and creating storage on each individual server, Server Manager allows an administrator to select multiple servers, view the available storage on each server, and then create a spanned logical share from the combined stored that resides on multiple systems

Windows PowerShell in Windows Server 2012 R2

Windows PowerShell came out several years ago and has since expanded from a command line utility that allowed organizations to script the creation of mailboxes in Microsoft Exchange to what PowerShell provides today which within Windows can be a complete end to end server build and configuration. PowerShell within Windows can be run locally or remotely, which organizations are finding Remote PowerShell being extremely helpful in running scripts to process server based tasks.

PowerShell within Windows Server 2012 R2

PowerShell can be used to create an entire virtual guest session from scratch, including building the virtual machine, setting the server name, IP Address, and adding server roles. Once the basic server is configured, a PowerShell script can configure server roles and features, ensuring that all servers are identically configured and setup with the appropriate security and configuration settings. After the server has been configured, PowerShell can be used to load application software like Microsoft Exchange, SharePoint, System Center, IIS Web Services, and even third party applications.

Ongoing configuration, maintenance, and support of a Windows Server can be performed through Remote PowerShell, kicking off configuration processes or making system changes across a handful, dozens, even hundreds of systems within seconds from a centralized location.

Understanding the PowerShell Deployment Toolkit (PDT)

One such tool that is helpful for datacenter administrators to get familiar with is the PowerShell Deployment Toolkit (PDT). PDT is a tool available for free download from Microsoft and is a fully scripted Windows Server and System Center 2012 R2 installation and configuration utility. PDT allows an organization to rapidly deploy something like System Center through a fully scripted installation.

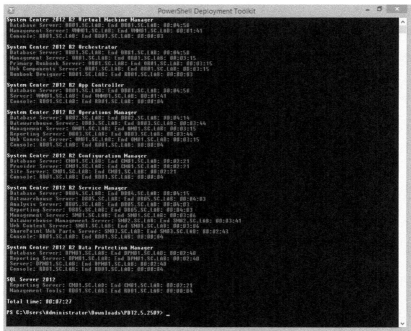

Microsoft's PowerShell Deployment Toolkit Scripted Installation

Rather than building System Center images from scratch, PDT simplifies the process in a script. For UNIX and Linux administrators within a datacenter familiar with Puppet and Chef that have scripted out the deployment of Linux applications servers for years, PDT will be a familiar type of process. Datacenters and enterprises looking to deploy multiple instances of System Center can leverage PDT to massively repeat the installation process with identically configured systems.

Remote Desktop Console in Windows Server 2012 R2

The Remote Desktop Console (RDC) has been around for a long time, formerly known as the Terminal Server console. Windows Server continues to support remote administration of a server system simply by taking control of the console of the server system. Administrators can remote into a Hyper-V host server and manage all of the virtual guest sessions running on the host server, or the administrator can remote into a single guest session and manage sessions one at a time.

Remote Desktop Console provides an administrator full access to the target system so that the administrator can add server roles, load system software, run a local administration console on the system, etc. Most administrators are familiar with the Remote Desktop Console for configuring systems; however more recently, administrators have been shifting their administration tasks to PowerShell-based tasks or through centralized application consoles.

Utilizing Application Consoles

Instead of managing and administering a single server through the Remote Desktop Console, there's been a movement toward the use of a centralized application administration console instead. Centralized application consoles allow an administrator to address all servers within an application, such as the Exchange Admin Center (EAC) that allows viewing, managing, and administering all Exchange servers in an enterprise. The Storage Spaces console within Server Manager centrally manages file storage across multiple servers in an enterprise, and the various System Center Consoles available allow for the administration of System Center management components for the enterprise.

Using Identical Policies for Patching and Updating On-premise and Azure-based VMs

One of the key goals in centralized administration and management is the ability to centrally patch and update systems with a common standard policy. And when an enterprise has virtual guest sessions on-premise as well as in Azure in the cloud, the virtual guest sessions are distributed and common policy management becomes even more important as systems are spread out across an enterprise and even outside of the enterprise's datacenter.

The good thing about stretching the enterprise datacenter to include Windows Azure virtual guest sessions is that the cloud-based sessions appear to be directly on the enterprise backbone and as such, the organization can more easily apply policies and ensure patching and updating remains the same for servers both on-premise and in the cloud. For organizations that don't connect all of their systems together, it's like managing multiple islands of systems and trying to maintain standard configurations.

Thus the movement is to interconnect guest sessions and apply common policies across all systems, both on-premise as well as in the cloud.

Using Windows Server Update Services (WSUS) to Update Systems

One of the free tools that Microsoft makes available to organizations is the Windows Server Update Service (WSUS) tool. WSUS allows an organization to create standard patching and updating policies and apply those policies to target systems. Update policies can be created across all systems, or systems can be grouped together for similar policies to be applied across common systems, such as across all Domain Controllers, or across all Exchange servers, or across all SQL servers.

Microsoft's Windows Server Update Services for Patching and Updating

WSUS centrally downloads patches and updates and brings them down to the enterprise, so that the same patch or update doesn't have to be downloaded from the Internet for each and every system individually. Instead, one copy can be brought down to a WSUS server, and all servers can access the WSUS server across the Local Area Network to acquire and apply the update.

WSUS also does centralized reporting, so that a report can be generated noting which systems have which patches and updates applied to it. The reporting system can identify deficiencies in updates, so that if the organization wants to ensure that a particular service pack is applied to all systems, the reporting can note which systems are lacking a desired update level.

Leveraging Microsoft System Center Configuration Manager to Keep Systems Updated

Beyond what Microsoft provides for free in the Windows Server Update Service tool, Microsoft also sells an update tool called System Center Configuration Manager, the current release is 2012 R2. SCCM 2012 R2 does what WSUS does in terms of identifying the patch and update level of systems, and will report on system update deficiencies. What SCCM does that WSUS doesn't do is enforce the update policy.

WSUS will identify which patches and updates have been approved to be applied to target systems, however it is up to the target system to download and apply the update. It is said to be a passive update system as the target system does the updating process.

With SCCM, the updating process is an active update process where the SCCM server pushes the update to the target systems, and the SCCM system can have the update forced to be installed and force the target system to be rebooted as well. While WSUS has to run a system scan to see which updates finally made it onto a target system and which updates have been applied, SCCM actively knows which updates have been applied, because it actively pushed the update and ensured the target system had the update installed.

Microsoft System Center Configuration Manager (SCCM)

Organizations that have tight regulatory compliance requirements tend to utilize SCCM, because SCCM actively keeps systems up to date and within compliance as determined by the organization. In an environment with WSUS implemented, a target system could choose to not install an update for some reason (potentially because a previous reboot hasn't taken place, or a 3rd party update is preventing another update from being installed), and an administrator may need to actively access the target system and enforce an update process.

Applying Compliance Settings in SCCM to Maintain Consistency of Configurations

When it comes to regulatory compliance, besides SCCM actively pushing updates, rebooting systems, and ensuring systems are up to date, SCCM also has a feature called "Compliance Settings", formerly known as Desired Configuration Manager (DCM). Compliance Settings allows an administrator to set standard configurations desired for a group of systems. All systems will maintain that certain level of configuration, and as such, a system will be patched up to a level and will be prevented from patching beyond a designated level unless the compliance setting is updated and changed.

This is important for anyone who has ever managed Domain Controllers or Exchange Servers or the like where all servers need to be on the same version of software and frequently the same Service Pack level as well as the same roll-up level. In an Exchange environment, if one server has Service Pack 1 and another server has Service Pack 3 with the latest Roll-up update, the user's experience accessing the two different servers commonly will be very different. Some versions of updates supported certain Web access features, while other version of Service Packs did not support certain Web access features. And the same applies for domain controllers, an environment with mixed versions of Windows for domain controllers may experience differences in logon access from users as it relates to Kerberos support, or encrypted password support, or server authentication support.

So it is important for many applications to not just ensure patches have been applied, but that a group of servers all run the exact same version of Windows, exact same version of Service Pack, exact same version of an application, and the exact same version of the application's service pack and roll-up. System Center Configuration Manager's Compliance Settings helps organizations ensure that systems in the environment have the same consistent configuration.

Utilizing Enterprise Standards for VMs On-premise and in the Cloud

With the right set of tools, an organization can ensure that all servers, domain controllers, Exchange servers, SQL servers, etc. on-premise are running the right version of Windows, Service Pack, and application update. But as the organization stretches to the cloud and starts to put workloads in the cloud, ensuring those systems are also of the exact same version, update, and application level becomes an important task for an enterprise.

Utilizing standards from the creation of the guest session using a template process or scripted process in the build of the system, through the ongoing maintenance and management of the system helps to ensure this consistency.

Thoughts and Questions

- Does your organization have a documented standard configuration desired for all systems and all system configurations?
- Do you used a scripted method or template method when installing guest sessions to ensure that all systems are configured the same from the beginning?
- Do you use WSUS or SCCM to patch and update systems, and conduct regular reporting to ensure systems are meeting the standards of the enterprise?
- Are you using something like SCCM's Compliance Settings to ensure that systems are configured the same, or if you are not, would something of this type help to maintain consistency of system versions across common server configurations?

8 AUTOMATING PROCESSES FOR A HYBRID ENVIRONMENT

One thing organizations frequently misunderstand is that putting virtual machines in a hosted cloud environment doesn't mean that the system never has to be monitored or managed. A virtual machine running in the cloud is no different than a virtual machine running on-premise. The system can still freeze up, get attacked by malware, lose connectivity due to networking problems, run out of memory and resources, and all of the other fun stuff that comes with server management.

The Server is in the Cloud, Why Isn't it Fully Managed?

When signing up for a cloud hosted environment, you want to determine whether the hosted provider is doing regular patching, maintenance, and even backup of the guest session for you. There's confusion in the marketplace between the various services being offered, and as such, validating the included services is important.

A decade ago, most of the outsourced datacenter providers typically included some level of patching, updating, and backing up of hosted server systems. Many small enterprises have popped up over the past half-decade in what is called "managed services" that also provide full patching, updating, and maintenance of servers.

However 3-4 years ago, a fork in the road came about that is different, and while fully managed servers still exist, a couple other paths have become available that are significantly cheaper in cost, and with that, comes different included-services.

Services for Platform as a Service and Software as a Service Environments

Two services that emerged a few years ago include Platform as a Service (PaaS) and Software as a Service (SaaS). PaaS typically is a service that provides a software development platform such as .NET development, or Java development, or the like where a customer builds their applications on the platform. The platform is typically patched and updated, so that part of the management is taken care of, but commonly PaaS providers do not provide backup or maintenance of the code. So it is up to the enterprise to ensure their code is backed up.

SaaS are things like Microsoft Outlook/Exchange in the cloud or SharePoint in the cloud within something like Microsoft's Office 365 hosted application services, or SalesForce.com or Box.net. These organizations provide patching and updating of the application so that all the user has to do is access the application and data. In these services, there are no servers to maintain or manage by the enterprise, and backups or archiving of information are part of the services.

What is included in Infrastructure as a Service?

The "other" branch in the past 3-4 years is Infrastructure as a Service (IaaS). IaaS has typically evolved to being a hosted hypervisor where an organization installs, configures, and manages their own virtual guest sessions. So the hypervisor is typically patched and updated, but the individual Windows or Linux guest sessions are completely the responsibility of the buyer of the IaaS service. The enterprise is responsible for patching their own systems, updating their applications on their systems, patching and managing the applications they have installed on their cloud-based guest sessions, and backing up their systems.

It's important to check what is included as part of the hosted services from the cloud provider, in the case of Windows Azure for guest virtual machines, Microsoft provides the hosted environment, but it is completely up to the organization to patch, maintain, manage, and backup the guest sessions. This is one of the key benefits that consumers of IaaS platforms find is that they own the systems and thus they don't have someone else accessing their applications, keeping backups of their applications, and all of the systems are managed still by the enterprise. The enterprise doesn't have to buy and manage hardware and racks of servers, but the enterprise maintains the responsibility (and ultimately the control and security of their application) that includes system updates, backup, and application administration.

Can I Get a Fully Managed Virtual Machine in the Cloud?

The question commonly comes up, can an enterprise buy a fully managed virtual machine in the cloud, and the answer is absolutely yes. There are organizations out there like Rackspace, Latisys, and hundreds of small hosters typically falling into the category of "managed service providers" that will provide regular IT services on guest sessions for a fee. For organizations looking to move guest sessions out of their datacenter and into a cloud provider, and have someone else patch, backup, and maintain the system, these services exist.

However, in the evolution of systems, organizations have to evaluate whether they want to continue to do things the "old way" by patching and maintaining systems, or whether other cloud hosted services might be best.

As an example, rather than moving Exchange and SharePoint to a managed service environment where your Exchange and SharePoint servers are running in a cloud-based datacenter, and then that cloud-based datacenter replicates your server to another datacenter for redundancy, and you pay someone to patch, maintain, and manage all of these servers for you; OR consider something like Microsoft's Office 365. Office 365 is a service where you simply pay a flat monthly fee for email, calendaring and file access, all connected to the latest Exchange and SharePoint servers on the backend, but you don't have to pay for the cost of the systems or systems maintenance at all. You just pay the monthly per user cost for the service.

Or, from a hosted guest session perspective, rather than paying a higher cost to pay someone to patch and manage your cloud-based guest sessions, which you internally still patch and manage your internal systems, you can just extend your ongoing internal management system to monitor and manage your guest sessions in the cloud.

What's Involved in Monitoring Virtual Machines in Azure?

That's the good part about network virtualization discussed in Chapter 6, that by stretching your on-premise datacenter to Windows Azure in the cloud, the virtual machines you have in Windows Azure look just like VMs on premise. So presuming you are monitoring and managing servers on-premise, with the stretched network to Azure, you can monitor and manage the cloud-based servers just the same.

The same monitoring policies and rules that you have in monitoring your on-premise servers, you can use to monitor your Windows Azure servers. When an on-premise server is down and someone in your organization gets alerted of an on-premise server outage, the monitoring of a Windows Azure server can run through the exact same workflow of alerting your I.T. personnel.

Managing Windows Azure VM Health from the Azure Console

Windows Azure's default management console provides a good snapshot of the health and performance metrics of a Windows Azure guest session. Information includes such things as CPU Time, Data In, Data Out, Server Requests, and service errors. The information can be displayed in hourly time increments or daily, showing a longer span of time. Within the dashboard view you can get a good sense of the overall state of the operating Azure virtual machine

Basic Windows Azure Monitoring and Performance Metrics

Leveraging Microsoft System Center Operations Manager for Enterprise Monitoring

Microsoft has a monitoring tool that is part of the System Center family of products. The monitoring component is called System Center Operations Manager (SCOM) and the current release is 2012 R2. Many organizations are already using System Center Configuration Manager (SCCM) for patching and updating systems or already own some of the licenses for System Center through the Microsoft Core Client Access License or Enterprise Client Access License agreements. So many organizations already own some of the licenses and/or are familiar with the System Center family of products, and as such, it has proven to be a good solution to leverage for enterprises.

Using SCOM to Monitor the State of On-premise and Azure Based Servers

System Center Operations Manager monitors server systems, and the latest SCOM 2012 R2 version monitors both Microsoft and Linux-based systems plus, with 3rd party plug-ins like the one from Veeam Software, can monitor VMware host servers and other 3rd party plug-ins that manage routers, switches, phone systems, non-Microsoft server applications, 3rd party SaaS providers, etc.

SCOM does traditional server monitoring to determine whether a server is running or not, plus it can also monitor common server statistics like processor utilization, memory utilization, disk input/output, network input/output, and the like. And there are "Management Packs" available from hardware vendors, free from organizations like Dell, HP, and IBM that will add specific monitoring attributes to determine the temperature of the servers, whether integrated storage adapters (i.e.: RAID controllers) are in a fault status, the health and status of blades within a server, etc.

There's a wealth of information that comes out of the management packs in SCOM that provides the health of a server system, and the management agents can be installed on servers both on-premise as well as on servers running on Windows Azure virtual machines.

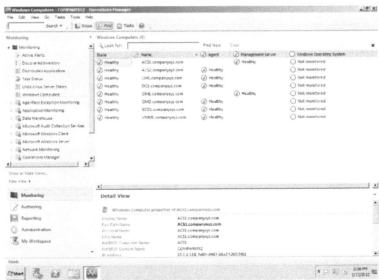

System Center Operations Manager Monitoring Console

As I noted that an agent needs to be installed, SCOM does provide agentless monitoring of servers, however with an agent installed on a system, you get a LOT more information about the health of a server, and agents commonly allow you to proactively manage and control a target server as well. So instead of passively looking at limited information from an agentless system, if you can install a SCOM agent on a server, you will find it to be much better in the overall process of identifying the state of a server and enacting a fix to the system, all from a centralized console.

Using SCOM to Monitor Applications Both On-premise and Running in Azure

System Center Operations Manager also has management packs for applications running on guest sessions, both on-premise as well as running in Windows Azure in the cloud. Typically no additional agent is required to be installed on the system; the same agent that was installed on the system to monitor the state of the server will typically report all of the pertinent information needed on the status of the application running on the system.

Application monitoring can monitor things like the performance and status of Microsoft Exchange, SharePoint, Domain Controllers, file servers, DHCP servers, DNS servers, IIS Web Servers, SQL servers, and there's a whole ecosystem of management packs available for non-Microsoft applications as well. Many of the non-Microsoft application management packs are available for free, some for a cost. Management packs exist for things like Oracle's databases, Sybase databases, Lotus Notes, and the like.

Also for application monitoring, an organization can not only monitor the server itself, but it can also monitor the state of the application from the perspective of users. Agents are installed on user-side systems and can conduct what is called Application Performance Monitoring (APM), where the state of the application is assessed, analyzed, and reported. As an example, an APM agent can determine that it normally takes 257-milliseconds to logon and get to a landing page on an application, but on a given date is now taking 750-milliseconds to perform the exact same tasks, which is three times longer. While the server itself might not be experiencing any performance issues, the user's experience can be 3 times slower, and as such, some form of trigger and notification will help the enterprise understand there is an application level error.

These types of monitoring of servers and applications can just as easily be monitored, tracked, and alerted on applications running on Windows Azure virtual machines as it would be running on an in-house server. And especially for organizations already running System Center for on-premise system and application management, monitoring and alerting on Windows Azure systems is just adding the Windows Azure endpoints to the SCOM monitoring console.

Extending SCOM Monitoring to Include Monitoring other Hosted Applications in the Cloud

For organizations that may be running applications outside of their on-premise datacenter or in Windows Azure, but completely outside of the enterprise like Salesforce.com, Workday, Box.net, Office 365, etc., System Center Operations Manager also allows monitoring of other hosted applications. From within the SCOM console, application performance monitoring can determine whether the hosted cloud providers are up, operating as expected, and any alerts and triggers can go back to the same enterprise console.

Monitoring Network Connections to Cloud-based Resources

With cloud-hosted services, whether it's a virtual guest session in Windows Azure or a cloud-hosted application, more and more enterprises are dependent upon the network connection to these cloud providers, typically through an Internet connection. If an internet connection is down, an organization can lose connectivity to emails, calendars, file systems, HR systems, everything. As such, being able to monitor the health and ongoing operational status of the connection to the cloud becomes important for the enterprise.

System Center Operations Manager provides monitoring of network connections, things as simple as the up/down state of the connection, but also the health of the appliance, router, internet modem, or other device that connects the organization to the Internet.

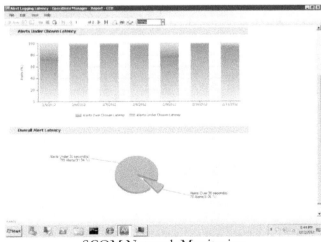

SCOM Network Monitoring

61

As more and more enterprises have a myriad of services in their enterprise, beyond just servers with applications running on them within the datacenter, it is helpful to have a centralized monitoring and management system to address in-house servers and applications, Windows Azure based servers and applications, cloud hosted applications, internetworking equipment communications, internet connections, networking appliances, etc., all under a common management platform.

Utilizing Real Time Alerting in SCOM

System Center Operations Manager provides real time monitoring as well as proactive event analysis and alerting. So in addition to identifying real-time that there is a problem and notifying you that something is down, SCOM will assess the ongoing state of systems and applications, and notify you that something isn't working in its normal state. As an example, if a system normally runs at 30% utilization but all of a sudden the system is running consistently at 80% utilization and is not dropping back, SCOM can be configured to issue an alert. Likewise, if you are monitoring 10 servers and all of the systems typically run at 25% and one of the systems is spiking at 90% while all of the other servers are still running at 25%, SCOM can be configured to issue an alert that one system is not working the same as others.

This real-time assessment and alerting helps organizations proactively identify and address problems before the situation causes a total system failure. Many times it is the conditions leading up to a failure that is indicative that a problem is pending, and SCOM can help organizations isolate and address the problems proactively.

Consolidating Alerts and Managing Events in SCOM

System Center Operations Manager also consolidates alerts and performs event correlation so rather than getting an alert that 50 systems on the other side of a WAN connection are down, SCOM can identify that the root cause problem is the WAN connection is down. This minimizes the number of alerts that an administrator receives, and thus allows the administrator to keep focused on the root cause rather than the ancillary problems resulting from the root cause event.

Additionally, SCOM can consolidate events from multiple systems into a common report and view. As an example, if an organization is looking for the password attempt logs across a dozen domain controllers in the environment, rather than manually exporting the logs out of each and every domain controller, the Audit Collection Service (ACS) feature of SCOM can gather all of the logs and produce a single common report.

Unlike many monitoring systems that treats systems as individual devices with alerts for each system, System Center Operations Manager can group together systems and treat them as a group of systems. This is commonly addressed when an organization might have say 4 Web servers load balanced to handle incoming communications; if 1 of the 4 systems is offline, rather than getting an alert in the middle of the night, if 3 of the systems are operational, SCOM can be set to suppress the alert until the morning so that the only time someone is paged and woken up in the middle of the night is when say 2 of 4 or definitely when 3 of 4 systems are offline. This is all configurable, and the administrators can determine what level of severity is associated with different states of failures within the environment.

System Center Operation Manager's ability to consolidate, manage, correlate, and prioritize alert notifications helps to minimize the constant paging and alerting that support personnel receive, and instead logically manages the alerts and issues urgent alerts only when urgency is necessary.

Producing Overall Enterprise Service Level Performance Reports

Besides just monitoring and issuing alerts, System Center Operations Manager provides reports that helps an organization understand the state of their environment. SCOM comes with dozens of built-in reports, and virtually any type of report desired can be created from the Report Generation capabilities in SCOM. SCOM 2012 R2 uses SQL Reporting Services that is extremely robust and customizable.

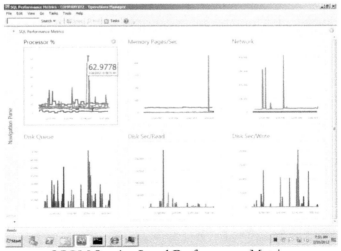

SCOM Service Level Performance Metrics

Some common reports are inventory reports, configuration reports, incorrect password attempt reports, high urgency event error reports, and the like. The reports can also be generated into graphics and displayed on a portal or displayed on a SharePoint page, providing the organization a snapshot view of system problems, service level response times, and overall health of the environment.

Thoughts and Questions

- Does your organization have a monitoring tool that monitors physical servers, virtual servers, applications, networking equipment, Internet connections, and cloud-hosted servers and applications from a central console?
- Would it be helpful using the same monitoring tool to monitor systems and applications on-premise as well as systems and applications running in the cloud?
- Would event correlation and system uptime notification simplify and help prioritize system health and operations?

9 ESTABLISHING THE BASE INFRASTRUCTURE FOR A HYBRID CLOUD

With an environment where you can build virtual machines on-premise or in the cloud, one of the common practices for organizations it to build a standard template for guest sessions that can be used across the hybrid environment. Microsoft provides a number of options for creating standard templates and build processes to ensure all systems are configured the same.

Using PowerShell to Create a Standard Virtual Machine Guest Session

As was covered in Chapter 7, "Managing Resources Both On-premise and in the Cloud," virtual guest sessions can be created using PowerShell scripts. For organizations that want to automate and simplify the process, PowerShell can be used to fully script the build process for a virtual guest session and configuration process.

PowerShell is a powerful tool for creating standard virtual machines and is of great interest to those who have been scripting the installation of guest sessions for years as the process is a command line process. However many organizations prefer to have a process that is more user friendly, based on a graphical user interface and with menus and self-service options for creating and deploying templates.

Leveraging System Center Virtual Machine Manager to Create a Standard System Template

For the graphical user interface solution with self-service virtual machine creation, Microsoft has as part of the System Center family of products their Virtual Machine Manager, or VMM. The current release of the component is System Center Virtual Machine Manager 2012 R2. VMM enables an organization to create templates for base configurations and store the templates in a library. The templates can be very basic Windows Server templates that have been fully patched and updated, or templates that already has server roles installed on them ready for configuration, all the way to templates that have applications already installed and ready for customization and configuration.

System Center Virtual Machine Manager (VMM) Console

Once a template has been created, the template can be stored in a library and called upon by subsequent VMM sessions to build a copy of the template and customize the template with unique server names, IP addresses, and configuration settings.

Enabling Self-Service Capabilities for Deploying Templates

For organizations that have templates created and want others to utilize the templates in the creation of guest sessions for themselves or their department, a self-service capability is built into Virtual Machine Manager. The self-service capability is assigned to a user by a VMM administrator to allow the user to utilize any or all of the templates in the creation of new systems. The administrator can issue a fixed amount of disk storage, fixed amount of processor capacity, and limit the total number of virtual guest sessions that a self-service user can utilize.

VMM Self Service Portal

Self-service functionality also automatically picks an available host system that has capacity in which to place the guest sessions, so that available resources are best utilized throughout the enterprise. This eliminates the need for the self-service user to make any decisions other than which template they would like to deploy and any configuration modifications they need for the system(s) they want to deploy.

Deploying Guest Sessions in Windows Azure from within System Center

As an organization creates guest sessions on-premise with System Center Virtual Machine Manager, Microsoft also provides the ability for an organization to use System Center to deploy guest sessions up in Windows Azure. Using the System Center component App Controller 2012 R2, an administrator can choose a Windows Server image to deploy in Azure.

The templates available in Windows Azure include the same type of templates organizations create on-premise such as Windows Server 2008 R2 systems, Windows Server 2012 systems, Windows Server 2012 R2 systems as well as systems with applications running on them. The application templates include systems running SharePoint 2013, SQL Server, or just simple Windows Servers running IIS Web Services.

Migrating Applications from On-Premise to Windows Azure

System Center App Controller can also manage the migration of guest sessions running on Hyper-V on-premise to be guest sessions running on Windows Azure. From within the App Controller console, an administrator can see both guest sessions running on-premise as well as guest sessions running in Windows Azure.

By selecting an on-premise guest session, the administrator can specify that the guest session be migrated to Windows Azure. Any configuration settings and system states can be moved across to Azure in the cloud, and the entire process can be done while retaining the on-premise system and configuration That way, an organization can migrate a system to Windows Azure, ensure that the application is working properly in the cloud, before retiring the guest session on-premise.

Using App Controller to View All Guest Sessions On-premise, in Azure, and in a Private Cloud Environment

System Center App Controller is a power tool that provides a single view of systems running on-premise, systems running in Windows Azure in the public cloud, as well as view systems that might be running in another organization owned and/or managed datacenter as a private cloud environment. In this day and age, organizations are no longer limited to just systems running in a single datacenter, and thus App Controller provides a single view of all enterprises resources.

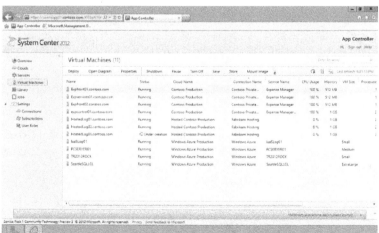

System Center App Controller Console

Utilizing Service Templates to Build Bundled Virtual Machine Configurations

When creating systems, it is rare these days for an organization to simply create a Windows Server or Linux Server guest session and be "done" with the installation. Once the server system is installed, the key is ensuring that an application is properly installed on the system, whether that application is IIS Web Services, SQL Server, SharePoint Server, or the like.

Additionally, it is rare for an organization to install all server instances in a single virtual guest image; as such, an organization deploying SharePoint will likely have a Web tier that has the frontend Web servers, and then have a backend tier of database servers holding system data. It is these two-tier or even three-tier configurations that make up the common deployment model for enterprise applications.

With multiple servers being the common configuration for applications, the build process needs to go beyond just building a single server image, but building out multiple servers, and having frontend Web services installed on some systems and backend database services on other systems.

Microsoft provides a solution called Service Templates within Virtual Machine Manager that allows a "bundle" of system templates to be configured together and then subsequently deployed as a template of multiple systems. The Service Template can have say 3 frontend Web servers, and 2 backend clustered SQL servers all configured as a single template. When the organization deploys one of these templates, all 5 systems are deployed at the same time.

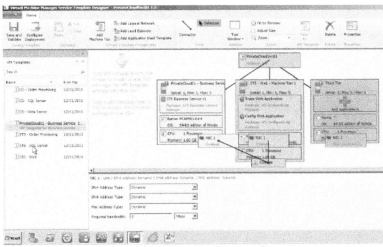

Service Templates in System Center

69

As the organization builds these Service Templates, a repeatable deployment with identical settings and configurations can be deployed. The administrators can make modifications to the Service Template and then redeploy the configuration again and again.

Expanding Automation Tasks Through the Use of System Center Orchestrator

Many times organizations have even more complex processes that are desired in automation, this is where the System Center Orchestrator component becomes a useful addition to the solution. Orchestrator is a runbook automation tool that can be triggered to run any of a number of tasks and sequences.

In the imaging process, many times an organization not only wants to build out a guest session with applications, but a special script needs to be launched to register software that'll be installed on the system, kick off a workflow task to harden the system and run it through security penetration and validation tests, also potentially through the process, email notifications need to go out to inform users that a system or series of systems have been configured.

Orchestrator is the tool that helps bridge the gap between what can be done within a base template and what might need to be launched and executed to do a lot of different tasks and sequences.

Utilizing System Center Orchestrator to Add System Capacity in Windows Azure

One of the creative uses of System Center Orchestrator is the ability for it to receive notification from System Center Operations Manager that the capacity of a running application is deficient and additional capacity needs to be built for the application. Rather than having the application run slowly until more hardware can be purchased and added to the network, a runbook in System Center Orchestrator can be launched that builds additional capacity in Windows Azure.

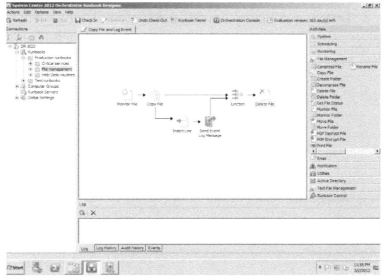

System Center Orchestrator – Runbook Automation

Since Windows Azure charges for running systems but not for systems that are shutdown, the organization can optimize its operational capacity by spinning up or shutting down systems based on demand. When the organization finally needs additional capacity in Windows Azure, the organization will begin paying for the available services when the systems are turned on. Orchestrator can be used to launch a script to build capacity through PowerShell, or launch a System Center App Controller request to build additional capacity in Azure.

If System Center Operations Manager identifies that the capacity is no longer needed, the guest session in Windows Azure can be shutdown, and the organization will stop paying for the running system.

This level of capacity growth and decrease is what provides organizations the flexibility and agility to expand into the cloud, and shrink back on-premise as needed. System Center Operations Manager identifies the need for capacity and automates the process to build more capacity as needed.

Thoughts and Questions

- Would a tool like System Center App Controller that provides a single view of guest sessions running on-premise, in other Private Cloud datacenters, and in Windows Azure in the public cloud help the organization best manage systems throughout the environment?
- Can automation tools like System Center Orchestrator be leveraged to

automatically have system capacity built on-premise or in Windows Azure as deemed necessary for the enterprise?

- Can a model where capacity is determined for system growth and system elimination help the organization optimize its use of cloud and on-premise resources?

10 CHOOSING AND MIGRATING THE FIRST WORKLOADS TO THE CLOUD

With the base infrastructure setup in the enterprise, someone needs to choose the first workload to place in Azure in the cloud. The workload can be an existing application or it could be a new application the organization is implementing that has never been installed on-premise and will be installed in Azure from the beginning.

The Simpler the First Experience the Better

When choosing the first application to install in Windows Azure, usually it is best to choose a very simple application, not try to put the most business critical, most complicated application up in the cloud in the first round. A simple first server to put in Windows Azure is commonly a single server, standalone type system. For many organizations, it might be their www public Web server as those servers are commonly single Web instances, potentially with an integrated database, but for the most part, a relatively simple Web system.

Other first server installations may include an organization's Intranet, a simple data entry system, or potentially an application server for a workgroup. These single node systems are easy to deploy, and typically easy to roll into and out of based on the tested experience of the application in the cloud.

If the application is merely known by its DNS address, a simple DNS change can point users to an in-house instance of the application, or it can point users to an external cloud-based version of the application. This DNS change can flip the connection state to an Azure cloud instance or back.

Building an Application from Scratch in Windows Azure

When a target application is identified, the organization can choose to build the application from scratch up in Windows Azure, or the organization can migrate the application to Azure, either way works fine. To build an application in Azure, since Azure allows the creation of common Windows Server or Linux host systems, the administrator can simply create a base operating system, and install the application on the system just as the organization had done previously on-premise.

Building a Guest Session within Windows Azure

If it takes an administrator 2-3 hours to build an application server on-premise, it would take no more than the same 2-3 hour timeframe to build the application in Windows Azure. Many times it is faster to build an application server up in Azure because Microsoft already has stock Windows Server templates that can be created in a few minutes, and since Azure doesn't require the building of servers, adding memory to a server, patching or updating a host system, all the administrator has to do is focus on generating a base operating system template and then deploy the application on the running guest session.

Migrating an On-premise Application to Windows Azure

Another option for an administrator is to simply take an existing running virtual guest session and migrate the guest session to Windows Azure. This can be done as a basic export of the guest session on-premise and an import into Windows Azure, or if System Center App Controller has been setup and integrated into the environment, the application migration can be conducted through App Controller.

Checking that the Application Runs in Azure without a Problem

Once an application has either been installed or migrated to Windows Azure, the application can be tested as an isolated instance. Even while the application is still running on-premise, the Windows Azure instance can be completely isolated and thus run and tested in parallel to the existing running application.

In this isolated configuration, an organization can test the application to see if all of the functions are working properly. Additionally, during this test process, some of the administrative tools in Azure can be explored such as taking a snapshot of an Azure guest session, adding monitoring agents to be able to monitor the Azure-based guest sessions, and testing remote administration and management of the cloud-based system.

All of these initial test processes can help an organization evaluate what it takes to deploy, manage, and support virtual guest sessions running in the cloud.

Switching a Test Session into a Production Session

If all it takes is a DNS setting to point from an in-house instance of an application to a Windows Azure instance of the application, then a DNS setting is all that needs to be configured to point to the cloud-based session. For most organizations, the switchover is done in seconds, and the organization is now "live" with the Windows Azure-based running system.

In some instances, firewall settings need to be configured on the Azure-based network connection which is a setting within the Windows Azure portal that opens up ports for connectivity to the Azure guest session. Most of this should be identified and tested during the testing process of a guest session, however sometimes that isn't identified and a quick firewall configuration change in the Azure Portal gets things working.

Choosing to Migrate a Multi-Server Application to Azure

Once an organization is comfortable with a single server instance running in Windows Azure, a more complex multi-server application can be installed, configured, or migrated to Azure. A multi-server application could be one of the template configurations mentioned previously that might be an IIS Web server frontend system with a separate SQL Server backend system. This two-tier configuration now requires 2 servers to be configured, and a network connection within Windows Azure to be configured so that the 2 independent guest sessions can talk to one another.

This is a distinction within Windows Azure that is different than typically building guest sessions on-premise. When an administrator builds a guest session on-premise, other guest sessions on the host server typically are all connected to one another the minute the guest sessions are created. This is because on-premise systems are typically fully accessible to networking the minute they are created.

With a Windows Azure guest session, security is enabled by default, and as such, EACH and every guest session is isolated from one another. Even if the Azure administrator creates multiple systems all at the same time, each system will by default be isolated and will not talk to one another. By configuring the networking on each Azure guest session, the systems can be interconnected to one another.

Alternately, for organizations that configure Network Virtualization and stretch their on-premise datacenter to include Windows Azure guest sessions in the cloud, once connected, all of the Azure virtual machines will be able to communicate with one another as well as communicate back to the on-premise datacenter.

Using Windows Azure for Test and Dev Scenarios

Beyond just the creation of simple virtual systems and multi-server application systems in Windows Azure, many organizations are using Windows Azure for Test and Dev scenarios. Rather than simply testing a single server for production, in a Test and Dev scenario, the organization may spin up dozens, if not hundreds, of virtual guest sessions up in Windows Azure.

In some environments, organizations are testing the installation process of an application they've created and want to test the operation of the application on various versions of Windows Server. In this example, the organization can spin up various Windows Server systems in Windows Azure, load up the software, and test the execution of the application. When the testing is completed, the organization can shut down the guest session. Microsoft only charges for the storage space the guest session takes up on disk, and the run time of the application. If the guest session is not running, there are no run time charges. And if the organization no longer needs the guest session itself, it can delete the guest session and thus not incur any incremental storage costs for the unneeded session.

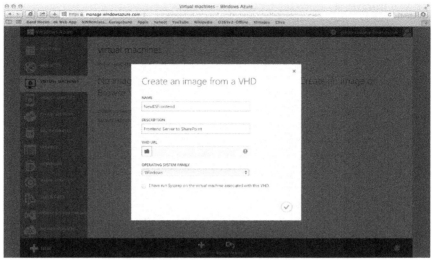

Importing a Virtual Machine into Windows Azure

And as an organization leverages Windows Azure for Test and Dev scenarios, the organization can infinitely scale their Test and Dev environment without any capital expenditure. During a launch release, the organization can test hundreds or thousands of virtual guest sessions for a handful of days, then delete all of the guest sessions and only incur a few days of expense. This drastically changes the cost structure in Test and Dev environments when an organization only pays for a few days of time than spending millions of dollars in capital purchases.

Handling the Conversion of an Old Windows-based Server to a Newer Server Configuration

Another common scenario for Windows Azure is organizations migrating applications off old on-premise servers to newer Windows Azure instances. As an example, an application may have been running on-premise on a Windows Server 2003 system where the hardware is out of warranty and is not very reliable. The organization can migrate the application onto a Windows 2008 R2 or Windows 2012 R2 underlying operating systems, test to make sure the application works fine on the new operating system and in the cloud; and with no capital expenditure, the organization can build, migrate, test, and ultimately run an application in production on a completely updated operating system, all hosted by Windows Azure in the cloud.

Thoughts and Questions

- Do you have a simple single node application that you can simply re-build in Windows Azure or migrate the application to Windows Azure to test and experience the operation of Azure for your enterprise?

- If all that is needed to switch an application instance from running on-premise to running in Windows Azure in the cloud is a DNS setting, would that be easy enough to try out Windows Azure, cutover the instance to Azure, and then cut back to the on-premise instance if there are any problems?

- Do you have a shortlist of the next 2, 3, or 4 applications that would be good candidates to move to Windows Azure?

- Do you currently do Test and Dev with physical on-premise hardware that you can potentially move the Test and Dev scenarios to leverage Windows Azure as the testing platform?

- Do you have Test and Dev applications running in other Cloud hosted environments that you can potentially move an instance or two into the new environment?

- Do you have applications running on old versions of Windows (i.e.: Windows Server 2003 or Windows Server 2008) that you can migrate the application to run on a Windows Azure-based Windows 2008 R2, Windows Server 2012, or even the latest Windows Server 2012 R2 base operating system?

11 INTEGRATING THE HYBRID CLOUD WITH OTHER CLOUD PROPERTIES

Once the enterprise has a successful implementation of a virtual guest session in Azure and has a hybrid environment with servers and applications running on-premise along with a virtual guest session or two running in Azure, the organization can look to integrate the hybrid cloud with other cloud services.

Integrating Active Directory with Other Cloud Services

As organizations implement cloud-based services in their environment, it's almost like taking a step back a couple decades to an environment where every server and every application required a separate logon and password. For the on-premise environment, it was Active Directory (and Novell NetWare and Banyan Vines before it) that provided a common directory for users and applications. However on a regular basis, we still see organizations not integrating their cloud services with their on-premise Active Directory and doing things the "hard way".

Pretty much every cloud provider supports single sign-on integration with Active Directory, it seems to be a minimum enterprise offering necessary for integration. Most cloud services allow for Microsoft's Active Directory Federation Service (ADFS) integration that effectively federates the on-premise Active Directory with the cloud service. ADFS focuses on the primary Active Directory authentication mechanism as the authoritative source and allows access to cloud applications.

Many organizations use third party directory integration solutions like Ping Identity, Okta, or OneLogin. These 3rd party solutions support standards like ADFS, OAuth, or they have a dedicated integration method that ties Active Directory to the cloud application for single sign-on authentication. The fewer times a user has to type in their credentials, and the fewer different credentials the user has to remember, the easier it is for a user to access resources. In addition to accessing resources with a common credential, if all of the credentials are tied to Active Directory and the individual leaves the organization, the Active Directory account can be disabled and the access to ALL integrated resources can be automatically blocked in the process.

Leveraging Microsoft's Azure Active Directory as an External Directory Service

For organizations that may want to leverage Microsoft's Active Directory in Azure, Microsoft provides a cloud-hosted directory. Azure Active Directory is used in a couple different manners. In one scenario, organizations use Azure Active Directory as the sole directory for the organization. Just as Active Directory on-premise is the primary authentication model for an organization, Azure Active Directory can be set as the primary logon point for users.

The other scenario that Azure Active Directory is used is for organizations that have external users needing access to content and information. Rather than placing external users in the organization's enterprise Active Directory, the users are placed in the external Azure Active Directory. Both the on-premise Active Directory and the external Azure Active Directory can be federated and point to a common application, like SharePoint, and thus users from both directories can access information. However, from a security perspective, the users are in completely separate directories and, as such, it creates a barrier between the directories.

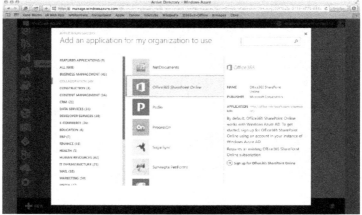

Windows Azure Active Directory Integration

Azure Active Directory is an Azure cloud service that has multiple uses and can be leveraged by an enterprise as a standalone service or integrated into a hybrid cloud configuration to create solutions for the enterprise.

Utilizing SharePoint in Azure for Shared Communications

Another Azure service that is available is SharePoint in Windows Azure. Microsoft provides the ability for an organization to run SharePoint document management, collaboration, and communications within a virtual machine in Windows Azure. So instead of an organization buying server hardware, configuring SharePoint on-premise, and managing internal and external users through internal firewalls, SharePoint can be installed, configured, and accessed in the cloud.

SharePoint in Azure is the exact same SharePoint 2013 that organizations install on-premise, so features and functions are the same. SharePoint in Azure just eliminates the enterprise's need to buy, maintain, and manage server hardware.

An organization can stretch their enterprise network to integrate the Windows Azure virtual machine that is hosted in Azure to connect SharePoint back to the enterprise network. This would effectively have the virtual guest session that SharePoint is installed on joined to the enterprise domain. As a joined system, all common SharePoint administration and management tasks as it relates to users, groups, and security roles follow the organization's Active Directory structure.

Conversely, an organization may want the SharePoint instance to NOT be part of the enterprise Active Directory, and instead use an instance of Azure Active Directory as the directory source for the SharePoint instance. This is commonly a good solution for an organization looking to host SharePoint that'll be accessed primarily from external users, and rather than tying the SharePoint instance to an internal Active Directory, the external instance of Azure Active Directory keeps a solid security boundary of users accessing the SharePoint content.

Microsoft provides server templates in Windows Azure that allows the simple deployment of SharePoint and the corresponding SQL backend database to be provisioned within Windows Azure. Instead of selecting a basic Windows Server template, an administrator can choose a SharePoint template and have SharePoint implemented in the cloud.

Supporting Hybrid Cloud Storage with Azure

Another common scenario in Windows Azure is the use of Azure for storage. As the cost of storage continues to rise, and the demand for storage grows exponentially, as organizations move to a fully digital environment, the need for a lower cost and simpler storage solution is desired by organizations. Microsoft provides storage in Windows Azure that allows organizations to store content in Azure. Content could be structured content such as a file storage space on an Azure virtual machine, where files can be written to the file system of an Azure VM. Or, Azure can be the target storage destination for information written to and through something like a Microsoft StorSimple appliance.

For structured storage space where an organization wants a cloud-based F> drive or K> drive type of setup, just a Windows Azure virtual machine running Windows Server can be setup as a target fileserver. With network virtualization and the enterprise's datacenter network stretched to Azure, the fileserver can appear just as any other fileserver that has been on the enterprise's network backbone for years. And with the instance of the fileserver residing in Azure, the organization can choose to open up the external port of the Azure fileserver instance and provide external access to file share resources.

One of the new technologies included in Windows Server 2012 R2 is Work Folders. Work Folders is an extension off of the traditional Windows fileserver system that now allows users to access fileserver content over HTTPS. So in addition to accessing fileserver content on the enterprise backbone as a file share, Work Folders allows content to be accessed and synchronized over traditional internet communication mechanisms.

Microsoft StorSimple Storage in Windows Azure

Microsoft acquired a company called StorSimple a few years ago and has integrated the appliance technology into its Windows Azure storage strategy. StorSimple is an appliance with local storage that can be set as an iSCSI target for organizations to write information to the StorSimple device. StorSimple ages content on the device and moves older and least used content up to Windows Azure, thus providing organizations an unlimited storage target system.

Because the StorSimple content is nothing more than a local storage target, the StorSimple appliance can be made as part of a traditional file system, where files and documents are stored to the system, or the StorSimple target can be used as an archive destination. StorSimple adds to the flexibility an organization has in terms of target storage, and one that has unlimited capacity as overflow information is written to Windows Azure.

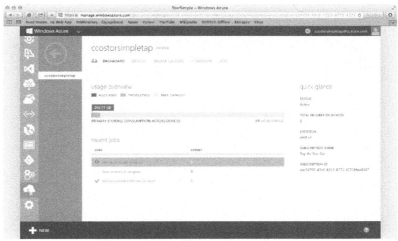

Microsoft StorSimple Azure Storage

Through the use of Windows Server 2012 R2 Storage Spaces, an organization can add a StorSimple appliance to a Storage Spaces share and utilize the storage on StorSimple and then into Windows Azure storage for virtually unlimited tiered storage. Storage Spaces spans content across multiple storage targets, with overflow content getting written to Windows Azure storage. This constant tiering of content provides real-time access to information regardless of whether it is stored on a traditional target storage system, locally on the StorSimple target storage system, or stored up in Windows Azure storage. A user never has to "think" about where their files reside, they just access a file share, and their data is viewable and accessible at any time.

Utilizing Apps in Azure

While we've addressed a number of hybrid cloud scenarios where Windows Azure extends the capabilities of the enterprise datacenter to the cloud, Microsoft also has its Microsoft's Azure Marketplace, where various industry applications are available for organizations. Applications are written by developers to address specific business needs or for specific industries.

Applications include simple things like time and billing tracking, timecard tracking, and document and note taking storage solutions. Other applications are industry-specific, providing solutions for healthcare patient management, government regulatory compliance management, legal industry case management, construction project management, and the like. There are hundreds of applications that organizations can purchase that run in Azure.

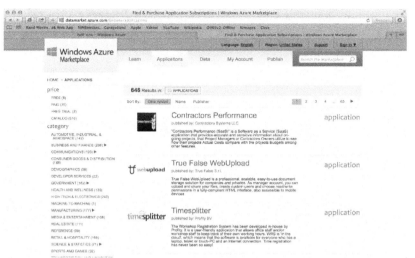

Windows Azure Marketplace for Azure-based 3rd Party Apps

Rather than buying an application and installing it on a local server or on multiple remote user systems, these Applications in Azure provide an organization cloud-based solutions for users. These applications are just an extension of an organization's business application space, and can provide an organization cloud-based functionality in parallel to existing applications run by the enterprise.

Provisioning and Deprovisioning Users Across the Enterprise

One of the important tasks for an enterprise is to ensure that only authorized individuals have access to critical business information. If an employee is terminated, their access to content should be blocked. This is the importance of single sign-on authentication so that when a user leaves the organization, their credentials like their Active Directory account, is disabled and thus their access to any application on-premise or in the cloud is blocked at that time.

The provisioning and deprovisioning of users can be easily integrated into Active Directory as long as the cloud-based solutions are also tied to the user's AD account. Workflows can be created in SharePoint or in System Center Service Manager that onboards a user and provisions the user's account and access; and then, when the individual is terminated, an automated deprovisioning process is launched, and their access to content is prohibited.

System Center Service Manager can leverage the automation structure of System Center Orchestrator to reach into applications such as SAP, PeopleSoft, Oracle Financials, Salesforce.com, Workday, or the like and have provisioning and deprovisioning tasks automatically triggered when an event in an employee manage system occurs. Connectors are available to interlink the various Microsoft automation tools to simplify the task of employee management in the enterprise.

Supporting Multiplatform Endpoints with a Hybrid Cloud Environment

And lastly, as organizations extend their enterprise datacenter to cloud-based services, at the same time organizations look to get better support for various endpoint devices that users use on a daily basis. This extends beyond the traditional Windows PC or laptop system and into devices like Apple Macs, iPads, Windows tablets, Android tablets, iPhones, Windows Mobile phones, Android phones, and the like.

In an environment where Bring Your Own Device (BYOD) is expanding throughout the enterprise with employees using their own phones and tablets and expecting to gain access to any of the information from anywhere, this multiplatform endpoint access to the hybrid cloud becomes more and more important.

Within the past year, Microsoft has actively started to acknowledge and support non-Windows based endpoints so that users with other devices have the same experience and same access to content as users on Windows based systems. For organizations leveraging the hybrid cloud, it is frequently suggested to upgrade servers and applications to the latest release of the products available, as the latest versions of server products have better support for various endpoints than older versions of servers and applications.

As an example, Exchange 2013 and SharePoint 2013 have excellent support for non-Windows endpoints and support any of the modern browsers for access to content; however earlier versions of Exchange and SharePoint have limited support and even greatly inferior support for access to content from non-Windows systems or non-Internet Explorer browsers. As noted earlier in this book, leveraging the cloud and rebuilding new versions of applications on new versions of operating systems in Windows Azure is an option for organizations and eliminates the need to buy more hardware or newer hardware, thus making the transition to newer systems a better option for the enterprise.

Thoughts and Questions

- Does the organization have an existing authentication application in use (i.e.: Ping, Okta, OneLogin) that it wants to leverage for single sign-on?
- With Active Directory Federation Services (ADFS) available free from Microsoft, will ADFS provide the necessary single sign-on capabilities to suit the needs of the organization?
- Can SharePoint in Windows Azure solve challenges for the organization in making SharePoint available to users both internal to the enterprise as well as external to the organization?
- Are there apps in the Azure Marketplace that can help the organization fulfill business application needs and eliminate the need for on-premise servers and on-premise applications?
- Can enterprise storage in the cloud assist in the growing demands of storage in your enterprise?
- Would a provisioning and deprovisioning process help your enterprise manage user access to content and block user access after their termination from the organization?

ABOUT THE AUTHORS

<u>Rand Morimoto, Ph.D., MBA, CISSP, MCITP:</u> Dr Morimoto is the President of Convergent Computing (CCO), a San Francisco Bay Area based strategy and technology consulting firm. CCO helps organizations development and fine tune their technology strategies, and then provide hands-on assistance planning, preparing, implementing, and supporting the technology infrastructures. CCO works with Microsoft and other industry leading hardware and software vendors in early adopter programs, gaining insight and hands-on expertise to the technologies far before they are released to the general public. CCO has had the opportunity to work with Microsoft Office 365 in such early adopter programs allowing experts and Rand to develop tips, tricks, and best practices based on lessons learned.

<u>Guy Yardeni, MCITP, CISSP, MVP:</u> Guy is an accomplished infrastructure architect, author and overall geek for hire. Guy has been working in the IT industry for over 15 years and has extensive experience designing, implementing and supporting enterprise technology solutions. Guy is an expert at connecting business requirements to technology solutions and driving to successful completion the technical details of the effort while maintaining overall goals and vision. Guy maintains a widely read technical blog at www.rdpfiles.com and is a Windows MVP.

<u>Chris Amaris, MCITP, MCTS, CISSP:</u> Chris is the chief technology officer and cofounder of Convergent Computing. He has more than 30 years' experience consulting for Fortune 500 companies, leading companies in the technology selection, architecture, design, and deployment of complex enterprise cloud integration projects. Chris specializes in leveraging Microsoft System Center to achieve high degree of on-premise to cloud integration, automation and self-service, reducing the level of effort and time-to-market for organizations while providing high levels of fault tolerance and availability.